DASHING DANDIES
The English hobby-horse craze of 1819

by

Roger Street

Artesius Publications

To The Dandy Chargers
"May your strides ever be long ones!"

First published in Great Britain in 2011 by
Artesius Publications

Copyright © Roger Street 2011

The right of Roger Street to be identified as author of this work has been asserted by him in accordance with the Copyright, Designs and Patents Act 1988

British Library Cataloguing in Publication Data
A catalogue record of this title is available from the British Library

ISBN 978-0-9532722-1-1

All rights reserved. No part of this publication may be reproduced, stored in a retrieval system, or transmitted, in any form or by any means, electronic, mechanical, photocopying, recording or otherwise, without the prior permission of the copyright holder.

Designed and printed in England by
Quorum Print Services Ltd
Units 3&4, Lansdown Industrial Estate, Gloucester Road,
Cheltenham. GL51 8PL

Contents

		Page
List of illustrations		iv
About the author		viii
Foreword		ix
Preface		xi
Chapter 1	Continental beginnings	1
Chapter 2	Denis Johnson, London coachmaker	13
Chapter 3	Hobby-horses by Johnson and others	21
Chapter 4	Johnson, son of Johnson	52
Chapter 5	The hobby-horse scene in England	64
Chapter 6	Matches against time, racing, accidents and prosecutions	76
Chapter 7	The demise and afterlife of the hobby-horse	90
Chapter 8	The Dandies and other riders	101
Chapter 9	Stage antics and Royal patronage	114
Chapter 10	Two and three-wheelers for the fair sex	129
Chapter 11	The hobby-horse prints	145
Chapter 12	Other velocipedes of the period	175
Appendix	John Fairburn's 'New Pedestrian Carriage' booklet	197
Index		213

List of Illustrations

		Page
Denis Johnson's patent specification drawing		Inside front cover
Fig. 1.	Army staff messenger on Laufmaschine	2
Fig. 2.	Laufmaschine illustration and photo	3
Fig. 3.	Karl von Drais on his machine	6
Fig. 4.	Karl von Drais c. 1820	7
Fig. 5.	Leipzig copy of von Drais' machine	8
Fig. 6.	Draisiennes dites Vélocipedes (print)	10
Fig. 7.	Draisienne horse brass	11
Fig. 8.	Marriage licence allegation	14
Fig. 9.	Signature of Denis Johnson	15
Fig. 10.	Stop him who can!! (print of Denis Johnson)	16
Fig. 11.	Horwood's Plan of the Cities of London, Westminster & Southwark	17
Fig. 12.	Denis Johnson commemorative plaque	18
Fig. 13.	Denis Johnson velocipede no. 204	22
Fig. 14.	Denis Johnson velocipede no. 204 (badge)	23
Fig. 15.	Denis Johnson velocipede no. 292	23
Fig. 16.	Denis Johnson velocipede no. 292 (side view)	24
Fig. 17.	Pedestrians Travelling on the New Invented Hobby-Horse! (print)	25
Fig. 18.	Every Man on his Perch, or Going to Hobby Fair (print)	27
Fig. 19.	Child's hobby-horse	28
Fig. 20.	Denis Johnson velocipede no. 100	30
Fig. 21.	Denis Johnson velocipede no. 100 (nose)	30
Fig. 22.	Denis Johnson velocipede no. 316	31
Fig. 23.	Jack Mounted on his Dandy Charger (print)	32
Fig. 24.	Denis Johnson velocipede no. 221	33
Fig. 25.	Hobby-horse (Canada Science & Technology Museum)	34
Fig. 26.	Denis Johnson velocipede no. 25	35

List of Illustrations

Fig. 27.	Denis Johnson velocipede no. 25 (nose)	36
Fig. 28.	Denis Johnson velocipede no. 25 (footrests)	36
Fig. 29.	Denis Johnson velocipede no. 31	37
Fig. 30.	Denis Johnson velocipede no. 31 (footrests)	38
Fig. 31.	Hobby-horse (Ipswich Museum)	39
Fig. 32.	Hobby-horse (Royal Museum of Scotland)	41
Fig. 33.	Johnson's Pedestrian Hobbyhorse Riding School (print)	42
Fig. 34.	Hobby-horse copy (Snowshill Manor)	44
Fig. 35.	Hobby-horse (Museum of Historic Cycling)	45
Fig. 36.	Hobby-horse (19th century photo)	45
Fig. 37.	Hobby-horse copy (Ulster Folk & Transport Museum)	46
Fig. 38.	Hobby-horse (St. John's Museum, Warwick)	47
Fig. 39.	Johnson, the First Rider on the Pedestrian Hobbyhorse (print)	53
Fig. 40.	Hobby-horse (Stockwood Park Museum, Luton)	59
Fig. 41.	Hobby-horse (Strangers' Hall Museum, Norwich)	60
Fig. 42.	Hobby-horses jockying the Mail!! (print)	67
Fig. 43.	Pedestrian Hobbyhorse (print)	68
Fig. 44.	Perambulators in Hyde Park! (print)	72
Fig. 45.	Modern Olympics (print)	78
Fig. 46.	Modern Pegasus or Dandy Hobbies in Full Speed (print)	80
Fig. 47.	The Female Race, or, Dandy Chargers running into Maiden head (print)	87
Fig. 48.	Military Hobbyhorse (print)	88
Fig. 49.	Non-steerable hobby-horse	94
Fig. 50.	Replica non-steerable hobby-horse	95
Fig. 51.	A meeting on the road (watercolour)	96
Fig. 52.	Mayfield family hobby-horse	97
Fig. 53.	Enamelled hobby-horse pill–box	103
Fig. 54.	A fob seal for the dandy's chain (two views)	103
Fig. 55.	The Dandies' Rout	106
Fig. 56.	The Right Hon. Robert Lowe M.P.	108
Fig. 57.	The Parson's Hobby - or - Comfort for a Welch Curate (print)	109
Fig. 58.	Silhouette of the Rev. Joseph Coltman on a velocipede	110
Fig. 59.	Dandy-horse playing card	112
Fig. 60.	My LORD *Humpy* Dandy!! (print)	115

Fig. 61.	The Perambulator or Pedestrian Hobby Horse (song cover)	118
Fig. 62.	New Reading – or – Shakspeare Improved (print)	120
Fig. 63.	Economy – or a Duke of Ten Thousand (print)	124
Fig. 64.	Staffordshire pottery jug	125
Fig. 65.	A P****e, Driving his Hobby, in HERDFORD!!! (print)	126
Fig. 66.	Willem, Prince of Orange's velocipede (two views)	127
Fig. 67.	FASHIONABLE EXERCISE, or The Ladies Hobby School (print)	130
Fig. 68.	Views of the Lady's Pedestrian Hobbyhorse (print)	132
Fig. 69.	Lady's hobby-horse (Science Museum, Wroughton)	134
Fig. 70.	Lady's hobby-horse ('beehive')	135
Fig. 71.	Lady's hobby-horse (arm & body rest)	136
Fig. 72.	The Ladies Hobby (print)	137
Fig. 73.	'Pilentum' plates	138
Fig. 74.	The *Hobby* Horse Dealer (print)	141
Fig. 75.	More Hobbies, or the Veloci Manipede (print)	142
Fig. 76.	The New Invented Sociable, or The Lover and his Hobby (print)	144
Fig. 77.	The Dandy Charger (print)	148
Fig. 78.	Match against Time or *Wood* beats Blood and Bone (print)	149
Fig. 79.	Going to the Races (print)	151
Fig. 80.	Anti-Dandy Infantry Triumphant (print)	152
Fig. 81.	Two-handled pottery jug	153
Fig. 82.	Every One His Hobby, plate 1 (print)	154
Fig. 83.	Every One His Hobby, plate 2 (print)	155
Fig. 84.	The Master of the Ordnance exercising his Hobby! (print)	156
Fig. 85.	Boarding School Hobbies! or Female Amusement! (print)	157
Fig. 86.	Man and woman on hobby-horses (watercolour)	158
Fig. 87.	Large commemorative hobby-horse jug	159
Fig. 88.	Enough to make a *Horse* Laugh! (print)	160
Fig. 89.	The Pedestrian Carriage, or Walking Accelerator (print)	163
Fig. 90.	Dandies on their Hobbies! (print)	164
Fig. 91.	Preliminary sketch for Dandies on their Hobbies!	165
Fig. 92.	A new Irish Jaunting Car (print)	166
Fig. 93.	Preliminary sketch for A new Irish Jaunting Car	167
Fig. 94.	The Chancellors Hobby, or More Taxes for John Bull (print)	168
Fig. 95.	The Devil alias Simon Pure (print)	170

List of Illustrations

Fig. 96.	Duke of Leinster's hobby-horse	172
Fig. 97.	Hobby-Horse Fair (print)	173
Fig. 98.	British Facilitator, or Travelling Car	176
Fig. 99.	Grinders (print) (lower and upper parts)	178
Fig. 100.	R***l HOBBY's!!! (print)	180
Fig. 101.	Manivelociter and Bivector	181
Fig. 102.	Trivector	182
Fig. 103.	Steam velocipedes	184
Fig. 104.	Hobby-horse with suspension spring (Hufstetler collection)	185
Fig. 105.	John Baynes' 'land punt'	188
Fig. 106.	Sievier's Patent Pedestrian Carriage (print)	190
Fig. 107.	Gompertz's modified Velocipede	192
Fig. 108.	Kent's Marine Velocipede	194
Fig. 109.	The Aquatic Tripod or Tricepede (print)	196

About the Author

Roger Street was until his partial retirement the senior partner in an old-established South Coast legal practice, but for about forty years his principal spare time interest has been veteran cycles and early cycling. He bought his first 'Ordinary' ('penny-farthing') bicycle in 1970 and soon became an avid collector of old bikes. In 1975 he formed the slightly quirky Christchurch Ramshackle Antique Bicycle Society – the CRABS – which is still going strong thirty-five years later. In 1979 his book *Victorian High Wheelers* was published – the story of an 'Ordinary' bicycle club which existed in Christchurch in the late Nineteenth century. In April 1985 Roger launched the world's first museum devoted solely to multi-wheeled machines, the Christchurch Tricycle Museum, which had over 100,000 visitors but sadly had to close in 1995. Over the past twenty-five years Roger has researched and written a number of articles for the national Veteran-Cycle Club magazine *The Boneshaker*, as well as preparing papers for the annual meeting of the International Cycling History Conference. His seminal work *The Pedestrian Hobby-Horse* was published in 1998. In 2001 he formed The Dandy Chargers, a group of Regency costumed riders of high quality replica hobby-horses who ride and demonstrate their machines at stately homes and elsewhere.

Fig. 29. Young Roger Street on his wooden horse: a Devon idyll

Foreword

by Prof. Dr. Hans-Erhard Lessing

'Two wheels replace four hooves' – such could have been the headline of German newspapers in 1817. Whilst the acerbic mockery, particularly in contemporary English prints, of the Dandies and their pursuits may have put off historians of technology, this important period of gestation in personal transport is nevertheless well worthy of investigation. Inventing a two-wheeled machine, the velocipede (known in England as the hobby-horse), was a serious problem-solving exercise for the individual concerned, Karl von Drais, who owned no coachmaker's works. The German inventor even had the sense to devise a rear wheel brake that could be applied gradually – a useful addition to the machine which was not adopted in England.

The reader might ask: why should there be a whole book on the manufacture of velocipedes by an English coachmaker (Denis Johnson) and related topics, when the hobby-horse era in this country only lasted for about three years. Well, for one thing, despite Johnson's patent, there were in fact several manufacturers who between them made perhaps as many as a thousand machines in the United Kingdom alone – and maybe more like ten thousand in Europe and America as a whole. Furthermore, the social history of the machine, its dispersal over a wide area, and eventual demise, is a fascinating story. And of course the hobby-horse velocipede is of seminal importance in the history of cycling, as half-a-century later it led on to the pedalled bicycle.

The "year without a summer" of 1816, caused by the super-colossal eruption of the Tambora volcano, has been rightly described by John D. Post as "the last great subsistence crisis in the Western world". There was a complete loss of harvest, resulting in famine, lack of fodder, and starved or slaughtered horses – especially in Germany and Switzerland. In this situation the invention of the velocipede was greeted like Columbus' egg, a brilliant idea which with hindsight seems simple, all the more since *homo automobilis* – self-propelling man – was faster than the mail coach! Pirated copies of the machine were made everywhere, although the requirement to balance was something of a deterrent to the majority of people not well versed in ice-skating.

Parisians often hired three-wheeled Draisines to carry their sweethearts around in the parks, imitating the hunting sleighs of the nobility. This explains the decorations of some velocipedes in Austria and France with allegorical animals heads, though these were not seen in England.

The subsequent demise of the velocipede can perhaps be partly explained by the fact that the first of a series of good harvests in the autumn of 1817 had closed the favourable window of opportunity for the invention in Germany, as horses came back on the scene. And in Germany the authorities had forbidden riding on the pavement or sidewalk as early as December 1817, forcing riders onto the rutted carriageways where it was almost impossible to balance. By the time the machine arrived in France in 1818, and in England in 1819, the famine of 1816 was largely forgotten.

Roger Street has done research for two decades and has collected source material on the early velocipede in the British Isles with remarkable success. He continues to report new finds at the annual International Cycling History Conference. No wonder his pioneering 1998 monograph of 195 pages required this revised edition of 220 pages, with many new so far unpublished illustrations and information.

Preface

> We have just now one of the prettiest of all hobbies … You may go at the rate of nine to ten miles an hour on a smooth road, with less fatigue than riding. They are making in great numbers … I am quite sure they are to turn out most useful things – you will observe they neither eat corn nor fall lame. *(Extract from letter dated 25th April 1819 written by James Loch in London to his brother in Bengal)*

The hobby-horse of the late Regency was a simple machine. In essence, it consisted of a beam or backbone supported by two wheels, with a seat for the rider and a handlebar for steering and balancing. An armrest was also usually provided. It was propelled by the rider pushing forward with his feet on the ground. It was of Continental origin, but was perfected in England, where for much of the year 1819 it "obtained a very general *footing* throughout the country".

The book's subtitle refers to 'the English hobby-horse craze of 1819'. The pedestrian hobby-horse was the archetypal bicycle. However, the bicycle proper only emerged in Paris some forty-five years later, when cranks and pedals were attached to the front wheel hub of a hobby-horse. And the word 'bicycle' only came into use half-a-century or so after the 1819 hobby-horse craze.

Although the hobby-horse era was a brief one, about eighty satirical and other prints were produced at the time in London. These are discussed in the penultimate chapter of the book, and there are a number of print illustrations. All the hobby-horse prints are to be reproduced in the author's proposed book *Before the Bicycle* (to be subtitled 'The Regency Hobby-Horse Prints').

This work is effectively a revised edition in a slightly different format of the author's 1998 book *The Pedestrian Hobby-Horse*, and includes new material which has come to light in the intervening years. The Appendix reproduces for the first time John Fairburn's *New Pedestrian Carriage*. This is undated but was probably written in April 1819. It is the only known booklet providing a contemporary account of the scene (another contemporary booklet, *Hobbyhorsiana*, is entirely fictional). The original is now owned by Lorne Shields of Canada, whose help with this book is much appreciated.

Chapter 1
Continental Beginnings

The hobby-horse story starts in Germany in 1817. To be precise on Thursday, 12th June 1817, in Mannheim. This was the date and place of the first recorded ride (of some nine miles) by its inventor Charles Frederic Christian Louis Baron Drais von Sauerbronn (Karl von Drais was the abbreviation he himself used).

Ackermann's *The Repository of Arts* for 1st February 1819 contains what is probably the first detailed note on the invention following its appearance in England. The writer states: "The inventor, Baron von Drais, travelled last summer [this should have read the summer before last] from Mannheim to the Swiss relay-house, and back again, a distance of four hours' journey by the posts, in one short hour; and he has lately [in fact, at the end of July 1817] with the improved machine, ascended the steep hill from Gernsbach to Baden, which generally requires two hours, in about an hour, and convinced a number of scientific amateurs on the occasion, of the great swiftness of this very interesting species of carriage."

Of course, in its country of origin the machine was not called a "hobby-horse". The first name given to it was a "Loda", which may be a combination of "lo" for locomotive and "da" for dada, the French word for a hobby-horse. The modern illustration is by Joachim Lessing (see Fig. 1).

In October 1817 von Drais produced a three-page advertising leaflet describing his invention, which he was now calling a "Laufmaschine" i.e. a "running machine". The well-known illustrations of a wavy-haired young rider, identifiable by his uniform as an army staff

Fig. 1. Army staff messenger on Laufmaschine, 1817 (Drais' advertising leaflet). Military use of the two-wheeler was contemplated at an early date.

messenger, are from this leaflet. Professor Dr. Hans-Erhard Lessing suggests that the contemporary French translation of this description substituting the word "Velocipede" (i.e. "quick foot") for "Laufmaschine" shows that the term "velocipede" was coined by von Drais himself.[1]

---

[1] However, it is possible that the word was known in Italy some years earlier – a Milan police ordinance of 1811, which cannot at present be dismissed as a forgery (although only a modern copy exists), purports to restrict the use of "velocipedi" within the city, on pain of confiscation of the machine.

Continental beginnings

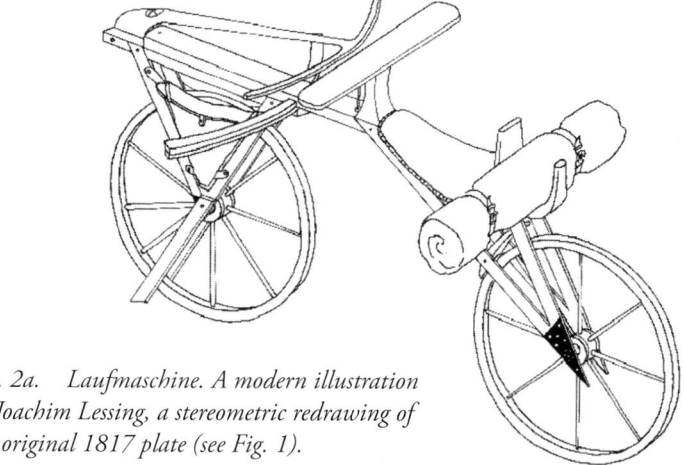

Fig. 2a. Laufmaschine. A modern illustration by Joachim Lessing, a stereometric redrawing of the original 1817 plate (see Fig. 1).

Fig. 2b. The photo by Tilman Wagenknecht, Erfurt, is of a machine at the Kutschenmuseum, Auerstedt. This was procured by von Drais himself from a cartwright in Mannheim in January 1818 for Grand-Duke Karl-August von Sachsen-Weimar, who gave it as a wedding present to his son. Both the saddle and the arm rest were height adjustable.

The definitive biographical work on Karl von Drais is Hans-Erhard Lessing's *Automobilität*, published in Leipzig in 2003[2]. Von Drais' early years were summarized by Hans Lessing in his paper *Karl von Drais' two-wheeler – what we know* read by him at the First International Conference of Cycling History in Glasgow in May 1990:

> Karl von Drais … was born in 1785 as the eldest child and only son of a leading official of the margrave of Badenia, in Karlsruhe, seat of the Badenian court. In those times the German speaking countries were split into a multitude of small political entities – with no national patent law at all! Presumably in opposition to his father, who had studied law and suffered from epilepsy, young Karl developed mechanical inventive skills. He had no easy boyhood – his mother died when he was fourteen, and before that the whole family had to flee the approaching French revolutionary army.
>
> Leaving school in 1800 he joined the private forestry school of his uncle and then studied physics and architecture at the University of Heidelberg for two years. In 1810 he was named Forstmeister (district forest officer), but was – with the help of his influential father – able to take paid leave! This worked well enough as long as his father lived, but later on the envious Badenian servants took revenge. The family had moved to Mannheim, also on the River Rhine; and Karl, now 25 years old, started inventing and publishing in the local newspapers.

The forerunner to von Drais' radically new Laufmaschine was his less original invention of a four-wheeled "Fahrmaschine" or "driving machine", for which he applied – and was refused – a Badenian privilege in 1813. There is no existing drawing of this machine, but von Drais described it as having a cranked rear axle driven directly by the rider's feet. The prototype was a tandem with the front rider

---

[2] Unfortunately, there is no English translation at present, although a biographical summary by Mick Hamer was published in the *New Scientist* for 29th January 2005 under the heading 'Brimstone and bicycles'.

steering the front wheels by two vertical struts – which could be let down to serve as shafts for a horse on steep hills, or in an emergency. The intended use of the vehicle was to provide: "summer spins for wealthy citizens, mail transport by keepers of post horses, war times transport of the wounded, transport of small loads."

Von Drais stated this machine could achieve a speed of two hours' walk within an hour, apparently meaning just four miles per hour, a modest but possibly accurate claim having regard to the poor state of the roads at that time. The reason why the inventor relinquished his first "carriage without horses" was stated by Fairburn, in his 1819 *New Pedestrian Carriage* booklet (reproduced in the Appendix), to be that "it required two servants to work it, and was a very complicated piece of workmanship, besides being heavy and expensive".

It appears that for the next few years von Drais abandoned the idea of land transport, concentrating on inventions such as a diving machine, a shooting machine and a method of speed writing. Professor Lessing suggests it may have been the volcanic eruption of the Tambora on the Little Sunda Islands in April, 1815, which indirectly inspired von Drais to invent his two-wheeled Laufmaschine. The eruption gave rise to a worldwide ecological catastrophe in the form of freak weather conditions, which in Germany in 1816 resulted in a bad harvest and famine causing some 40,000 people to emigrate. As Adam Smith had written earlier, did it make sense to feed horses for transport when people were starving? If we accept this theory, it suggests that von Drais may have been planning his new machine for up to a year before it actually took to the road.

If a volcanic eruption may have produced the *motivation* for a new machine, it is likely that the actual *inspiration* was the activity of ice skating. In his advertising leaflet of October 1817[3] von Drais states: "On a hard road, the rapidity of the Velocipede resembles that of an

---

[3] Translated in the *Birmingham Commercial Herald* for 20th March 1819.

Fig. 3. Karl von Drais on his machine, 1819 (courtesy of Städt. Reiss-Museum, Mannheim). Until recently, this was thought to be the only authentic contemporary picture of the inventor.

Fig. 4. Karl von Drais c.1820 (courtesy of Dr. Michael Friedmann). This has only relatively recently been confirmed by Professor Hans Lessing as being a portrait of the German inventor.

expert skaiter; as the principles of the two motions are the same. In truth, it runs a considerable distance while the rider is inactive, and with the same rapidity as when his feet are in motion". An English newspaper puts it more succinctly the following year: "The principle of the invention is taken from the *Art of Skaiting*"[4].

The following limerick by the present author not only records the supposed inspirational moment, but also aims to assist English speakers with the correct pronunciation of the inventor's name:-

> There once was a Baron von Drais [pronounced 'Drice']
> Who observed some swift skaters on ice
> "If they balance on steels
> Then why not two wheels –
> Yes, a Laufmaschine, that would be nice!"

---

[4] *The Courier*, 11th December 1818.

Fig. 5. Leipzig machine. One of a number of unauthorized, albeit modified, copies of von Drais' machine. Note the simplified steering arrangement, also the capacious luggage-carrying baskets. The bonnets are rather fetching, and similar fashions would have been worn in England by the dandizettes (female dandies).

Von Drais' application in 1817 for a Badenian privilege was granted in January 1818. He also applied through his servant Louis for a patent in France, which was duly granted in February of the same year. In late March the machine was being tried out in the Luxembourg Gardens in Paris, where it "manoeuvred with great rapidity"[5].

A week or so later, the machine was again being exhibited in the Luxembourg Gardens. This event was described in the *Liverpool Mercury*, under the heading "CARRIAGES WITHOUT HORSES (From the Paris papers)" in the following terms:-

> An immense concourse of spectators assembled yesterday [5th April 1818] at noon, at Luxemburg, to witness the experiments with <u>Draisiennes</u> (a species of carriage moved by machinery without horses). The crowd was so great that the experiments were but imperfectly made. The machine went, however, quicker than a man running at speed, and the conductors did not appear fatigued.
>
> About three, a lady appeared in a Draisienne, conducted by the chasseur [huntsman] of the Baron de Drais, who made with it several turns in the alleys, in the midst of the crowd. The machine, although charged with a double weight, had the same rapidity, and the efforts of the conductor did not seem to be increased. The machine ascended with facility the hillocks which are placed in some parts of the garden.
>
> The Draisiennes appear to be convenient for the country, and for short journies on good roads.[6]

The French print *Draisiennes dites Vélocipèdes* apparently dates from April 1818 (see Fig. 6). It depicts (translating from the French inscription) "portable and economic horses invented outside France". The Bibliotheque Nationale catalogue of prints describes the scene (again translating from the French) as a "German velocipedist guided by

---

[5] According to a report in the *Salisbury and Winchester Journal* for 6th April 1819.
[6] 24th April 1818.

Fig. 6. 'Draisiennes dites Vélocipèdes' (author's collection). An interesting if somewhat puzzling print. Who was the rider? Why was he armed with two pistols and a sword? Who was the second rider, only hinted at in the picture? And why the goose?!

Fig. 7. Draisienne horse brass (author's collection). A modern horse brass struck in 1976 to commemorate the twenty-first anniversary of the formation of the Southern Veteran-Cycle Club (now the Veteran-Cycle Club).

a goose". In view of the date it seems reasonable to speculate that the individual caricatured may be the servant of Karl von Drais, followed by another rider, venturing beyond Paris into the open countryside[7].

In October 1818 Drais himself travelled to France and demonstrated his velocipede in both Nancy and Paris[8]. It seems likely that

---

[7] The 'Poste aux Chevaux' archway does not imply a connection with the French Post Office, a 'Post House' was a feature of a 'stately home'. One can still be seen at Les Ormes, which has a grand archway with the same wording leading to a large courtyard with stabling and other related buildings around it.

[8] A detailed English description of the impact of the Draisienne in France, and elsewhere in Europe, is contained in *On Your Bicycle* by James McGurn (second edition 1999, in the section 'The Running Machine').

he returned to Paris in 1830 to promote the use of his machine by the French rural postmen, with only limited success[9].

Von Drais died aged 66 years on 12th October 1851. More than forty years later, in 1893, a monument was erected to his memory at his birthplace, Karlsruhe, by the German Bicyclists Union.

There is an interesting reference to the use of an English made Laufmaschine in a lecture given by Thomas Davies (original in Trinity College Library) in May 1837:-

> Soon after the publication of [the von Drais advertising pamphlet], a German gentleman with whom I was acquainted, named Mr. Bernhard Seine, a native of the City of Mannheim, came to England, about twenty years ago, bringing with him the pamphlet, and he frequently rode about the streets of the City of Bath upon a velocipede made after the construction of the original invention. Mr. Seine did not hesitate to run on his velocipede at a violent rate down some of the steepest streets in that city over the pitching of the road, but I never heard of his meeting with any accident.

---

[9] Unpublished paper by the author entitled 'The Mysterious Monsieur Dreuze'.

Chapter 2
Denis Johnson, London coachmaker

Herr Bernhard Seine may have been England's first velocipedist. But the real credit for introducing the machine into this country belongs wholly and solely to another individual, a coachmaker of Long Acre in the City of Westminster, Denis Johnson. At present we know relatively little of his early life, despite the primary importance of his role in connection with the development of the English pedestrian hobby-horse. Regrettably, the majority of the early records of the Worshipful Company of Coachmakers and Coach Harness Makers were destroyed during the Second World War, and those that remain at the Guildhall Library, London, contain no reference to Johnson.

All the currently available information is contained in an article on Johnson in the *Oxford Dictionary of National Biography*[10].

Johnson's stated age at death suggests he was born in 1760, but as yet we have no knowledge of his place or exact date of birth. Denis Johnson married Mary Newman by licence of the Archbishop of Canterbury at St. Anne's parish church, Soho (the bridegroom's parish), in the City of Westminster, on Friday, 17th February, 1792, when he would have been 31 or 32 years old. The application for the licence was made by Denis's fiancée, as the illustrated marriage allegation shows (see Fig. 8). Neither party had previously been married. Why the couple decided to pay a fee to avoid publication

---

[10] Oxford University Press, 2004.

of banns in their parish churches, why the application was to the archbishop as opposed to the bishop or archdeacon of the diocese, why Mary and not Denis made the allegation (and provided a bond against any "lawful impediment"), must for the moment remain matters for conjecture.

Denis and Mary had two daughters, Mary and Ann, born in 1795 and 1798 respectively. The family lived in Soho for a number of years, certainly until the turn of the century. Presumably Denis was working as a coachmaker, though as yet we have no proof of this.

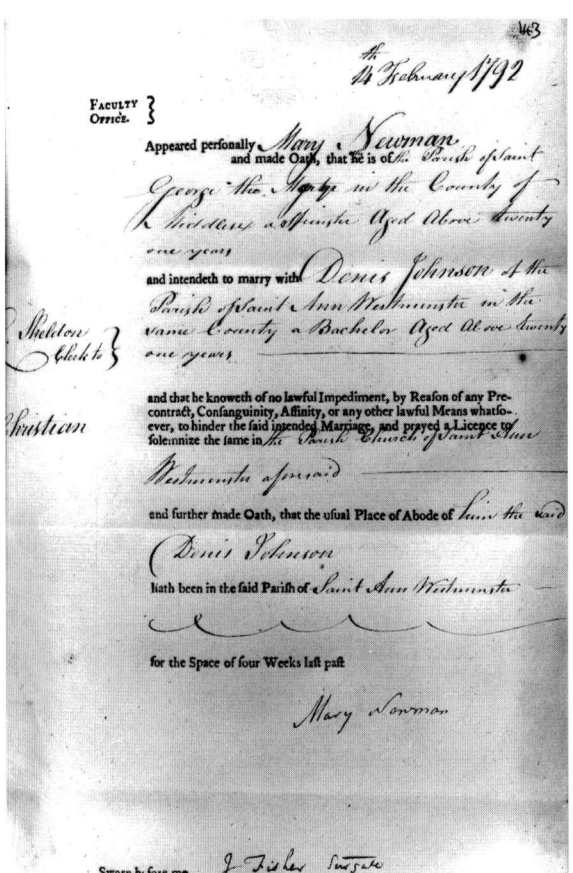

Fig. 8. Marriage licence allegation, 1792 (courtesy of Lambeth Palace Library, London). The licence itself was granted the same day as the allegation (and bond) – St. Valentine's Day, 14th February 1792. The marriage between Denis Johnson and Mary Newman took place three days later.

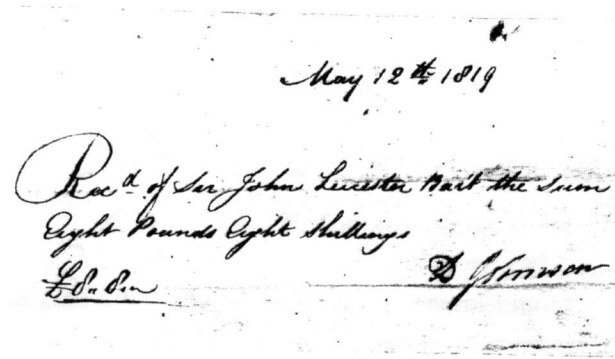

Fig. 9. Receipt with signature of Denis Johnson (reproduced by courtesy of the University of Manchester). An account also in Johnson's hand confirms the payment is for "a New Patent Pedestrian Machine".

In Holden's *Triennial Directory for 1799* Johnson has no entry in the business section, but is listed as having a private address in Bateman's Buildings, a narrow thoroughfare immediately to the south of Soho Square (then known as King Square), where he is recorded as paying the usual householder rates. Johnson also had an illegitimate son, John Johnson (date of birth unknown), of whom we shall hear more later.

Denis Johnson was in his late fifties when von Drais invented his Laufmaschine, which became known as the Draisienne in France and was soon heard of in England. Johnson's known age seems to tie in with the only known image we have of him, in the 1819 print (see Fig. 10) *Stop him who can!! An English patentee introducing a French hobby-horse – or a bit of a push down Highgate-Hill to Long Acre.*

As a result of a search in the Tabley House papers in the John Rylands Library, Manchester,[11] we have examples (see Fig. 9) of Denis Johnson's businesslike handwriting and signature. Although there is a gap of more than quarter of a century, Johnson's 1792 signature in the St. Anne's marriage register is very similar to those of the Tabley House receipts.

---

[11] Reported to Glynn Stockdale of the Veteran-Cycle Club.

Dashing Dandies

Fig. 10. 'Stop him who can!!', 1819 print (courtesy of the Pryor Dodge Collection). Although it was Johnson's son who was the skilled velocipedist, this depiction of Denis Johnson himself on a machine causing mayhem on Highgate Hill seems unjustified. If the artist is Cruikshank, he may well be recalling his own escapade on the same hill described in Chapter 11. Note absence of arm rest — a machine ridden by Johnson would in reality have had one.

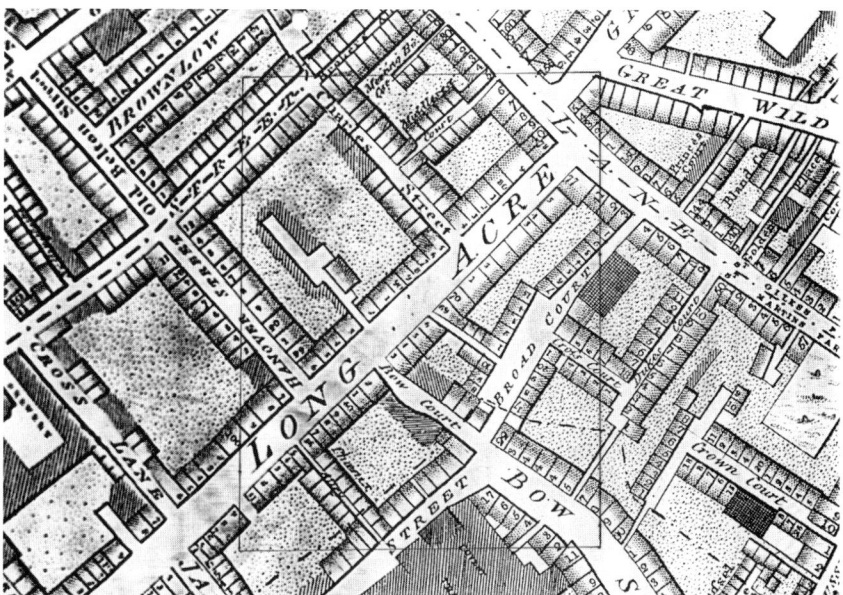

Fig. 11. Horwood's 'Plan of the Cities of London, Westminster & Southwark' (courtesy of Westminster Archives Centre, London). As can be seen, Johnson's premises at 75 Long Acre occupied one of the larger sites.

The rating records for the parish of St. Martins-in-the-Fields show that Johnson took occupation of 75 Long Acre in March 1818[12]. An extract from Horwood's *Plan of the Cities of London, Westminster and Southwark* shows the street layout in Johnson's day, little altered at the present time (see Fig. 11). No. 75 adjoins the property on the corner of Long Acre and Drury Lane (the parish and city boundary). The site of the long-demolished premises is now part of Acre House, 69-76 Long Acre, a late Nineteenth century building. At the author's suggestion, the Covent Garden Area Trust applied to the City of Westminster for the Council to erect a plaque on the present building, to record that this is the site of Denis Johnson's workshop (see Fig. 12).[13]

---

[12] The year is also confirmed by the London trade directories.
[13] The plaque was unveiled on 2nd July 1998 by the then Sports Minister, Tony Banks.

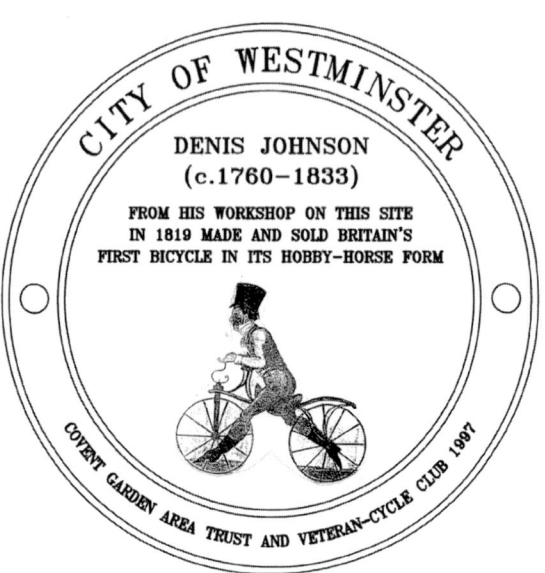

Fig. 12. Denis Johnson commemorative plaque. A fitting and permanent memorial at 75 Long Acre to the maker of 'Britain's first bicycle' in its hobby-horse form.

We do not know exactly how Johnson became aware of the von Drais machine, but we do know that this was his inspiration for devising a more attractive and streamlined version of his own. And it must surely have been Denis Johnson who was the "ingenious coach-builder of this metropolis" who was said to have "procured one of these useful machines, in which he expects to make some important improvements"[14]. As a coachmaker, Johnson was able to use his professional skills to improve the German machine, particularly by substituting metal for wood where he thought it appropriate to do so.

It was probably in the autumn of 1818 (the exact date is not known) that Johnson applied by Petition to be granted a Patent. There appears to be no copy of the Petition (or of the required law officer's Report) in existence, although the document is referred to in a Warrant dated

---

[14] *The Courier*, 11th December 1818, under the heading 'Newly-Invented Carriage'.

6th November 1818 and in a Bill dated 11th December 1818, both leading to the Grant of the Patent[15]. According to a contemporary German newspaper[16], the patent cost was the then not inconsiderable sum of £100.

A complete copy of the Grant to Denis Johnson of Royal Letters Patent dated 22nd December 1818[17] can be seen on a patent roll at the National Archives at Kew[18].

It commences as follows:

> GEORGE the Third by the Grace of God etc. To all to whom these Presents shall come Greeting Whereas Denis Johnson of 75 Long Acre in the Parish of Saint Martin in the Fields in the County of Middlesex Coachmaker hath by his Petition humbly represented unto us that in consequence of a Communication made to him by a certain Foreigner residing abroad he is become possessed of a certain invention of a Machine for the purpose of diminishing the labour and fatigue of persons in walking and enabling them at the same time to use greater speed which said Machine he intends calling the Pedestrian Curricle That the said invention or machine is new in this kingdom and hath not been practiced therein by any other person or persons whatsoever to his knowledge or belief …

We do not have the name of the "certain Foreigner residing abroad" who communicated the invention to the London coachmaker. Could it have been von Drais himself? This seems unlikely though it cannot at this stage be ruled out as a possibility. Karl von Drais applied outside Germany for patents in Austria (unsuccessfully) and France (successfully), and if he had wanted to could presumably have done so through an agent in England. There is no evidence of any arrangement between Johnson and von Drais, under which the

---

[15] National Archives references HO 89/9 and SO 7/306.
[16] *Oppositions-Blatt oder Weimarische Zeitung.*
[17] Number 4321 of 1818.
[18] Reference C66/4205.

German inventor agreed to the English coachmaker proceeding with a patent application in his own name, in consideration of financial recompense.

The Grant of Patent was for a term of fourteen years, and gave Johnson six months to provide full details of his invention. This he did just in time, the Specification (with drawings) being dated and inrolled on 21st June 1819[19].

The Specification allows for the seat of the machine to be adjustable, also (like the Draisienne) there is a rest for the rider's elbows and forearms "so as to support himself with the full muscular use of his legs". An important sentence appears towards the end of the document: "The dimensions of this machine must depend upon the height and weight of the person who is to use it, as well as the materials of which it may be formed, consequently no specific directions can be given about them, further than saying that the lighter and more free from friction the whole can be made, and the larger the diameter of the wheels, the better and more expeditious the machine will be".

---

[19] National Archives reference C54/9824.

Chapter 3
Hobby-horses by Johnson and others

In the patent specification drawings (and in many of the prints) the front and rear wheels appear to be the same size, but some surviving machines have a rear wheel slightly larger than the front one. For example, the Science Museum's gentleman's hobby-horse has a 25½" diameter front wheel and a 27" rear wheel. Most known examples have ten spokes per wheel (two have twelve). The twelve known existing Johnson gentleman's machines are of varying sizes, and were no doubt supplied in accordance with the requirements of individual purchasers. A recently discovered 'Johnson' in the Pitt Rivers Museum at Oxford University (see Fig. 15 and Fig. 16) has just 22¾" front and rear wheels, and may have been a youth's machine.

Several of the surviving machines have either a simple metal rod stand, or two holes in the beam where one could be fitted, for use when the machine is not being ridden. No known Johnson velocipede has or had a brake fitted, even though von Drais had allowed for one on his Laufmaschine.

Most of the existing Johnson hobby-horses have his brass oval nameplate on the front of the steering handle, stating "JOHNSON'S PATENT" above the Royal Coat of Arms, with his address "75 LONG ACRE LONDON" underneath, as shown in the photo illustration of the Science Museum, Wroughton, gentleman's machine (see Fig. 13 and Fig. 14). In all examples, the steering bar is above a brass dome, the inspiration for which has been said to be the nearby

Fig. 13.   Denis Johnson velocipede no. 204 (photo courtesy of Science Museum, Wroughton). Note straight handle, direct steering bar and arm rest with four supports.

Fig. 14. Denis Johnson velocipede no. 204 (photo courtesy of Science Museum, Wroughton). Johnson's name plate, despite being worn and cracked, is still an attractive item.

Fig. 15. Denis Johnson velocipede no. 292 (photo courtesy of the University of Oxford). A recently discovered machine. The smallest known Johnson hobby-horse.

Fig. 16.   Denis Johnson velocipede no. 292 (photo courtesy of the University of Oxford). Side view. Note the broken arm rest support bar.

dome of St. Paul's cathedral, and in a couple of cases there is a brass leafy ornament at the front and rear of the main beam. Some of the surviving machines also have a piece of ornamental metalwork bridging the dome.

In contemporary literature, the weight of the manufactured item was commonly given as about fifty pounds, though some of the surviving examples weigh considerably less than this. The Pitt Rivers Museum hobby-horse weighs just 37½ pounds.

It seems that, in addition to his two-wheelers, Denis Johnson also made a three-wheeler. This is shown in the print *Pedestrians travelling on the New Invented Hobby horse!* published by Sidebethem in 1819, the artist/engraver being Robert Cruikshank (see Fig. 17). Another Cruikshank print, *Dandies on their Hobbies!*, (see Fig. 90), also shows three-wheeled hobby-horses, the machines in this case also having a seat for a lady passenger.

Hobby-horses by Johnson and others

Fig. 17. 'Pedestrians Travelling on the New Invented Hobby-Horse' (1819 print, author's collection). An important item depicting a Johnson three-wheeler. Note the foreground rider's travelling box and back-pack.

25

As can be seen from the prints, the two rear wheels are relatively close together, and the suggestion is that the machine was simply intended to provide an aid to balancing, rather than create a tricycle as we would understand the word today.

What seems fairly certain is that such machines were actually made, as the hobby-horse print artist is unlikely to have depicted this relatively small but important variation of the Johnson item if it had not in fact existed. This is confirmed by a letter in the archives of the Rhode Island Historical Society, apparently written by William A. Robinson on 29th June 1819, possibly from England to a relative in Rhode Island, America. It contains an accurate sketch of a Denis Johnson machine. The writer states: "It represents and is intended to represent one with <u>two</u> wheels ... There are some made with three wheels – two behind and one before. ... I think those with three wheels preferable for good roads, as they require no care to keep them upright which those with only two do."

Some imaginary three-wheeled hobby-horses are featured in the Robert Cruikshank print *Every Man on his Perch, or Going to Hobby Fair*, published by G. Humphrey dated 10th July 1819 (see Fig. 18). But taking a different line to William Robinson, a certain 'E.B.', writing at some length in the *Monthly Magazine* for July 1819, describes the two-wheeler as "a very superior mode of exercise", and adds "I do not believe those of two wheels behind will answer, as they would require very great exertion".

A Liverpool advertisement by Johnson under the heading 'Modern Recreation'[20] refers to "A Machine for the use of Young Gentlemen from the age of 12 years, as recommended by the Faculty, is arrived from London".

What may just possibly be a child's machine by Johnson (though there is no nameplate or visible number) is shown in Fig. 19. Both

---

[20] *Liverpool Mercury*, 4th June 1819.

Hobby-horses by Johnson and others

Fig. 18. 'Every Man on his Perch', of Going to Hobby Fair' (1819 print, courtesy of Lewis Walpole Library, Yale University). Three of the hobby-horse riders are depicted on imaginary three-wheelers appropriate to their trades.

27

Fig. 19. Child's hobby-horse (Worthing Museum). A unique machine, by or after Johnson.

wheels have a diameter of 18½".[21] At the front end of the main beam is a small silver crest of a cubit arm in armour holding a cutlass. According to the College of Arms in London, this is identifiable with the Seventeenth century Beadle family of Essex, and it may be that the child's hobby-horse belonged to a descendant.

Denis Johnson used Roman numerals to number his machines, presumably on a consecutive chronological basis. The Account Book of the House Steward of the Third Duke of Northumberland contains a payment item for 26th May 1819: "Bill for new pedestrian machines 22 – -" i.e. £22. This clearly relates to the Duke's two machines numbered 299 and 300, which to this day remain at the family home at Alnwick Castle.

Sir John Leicester of Tabley House also bought two machines, the receipts for which are dated 1st April and 12th May 1819 respectively. As far as we know, the only machine now remaining is the one bearing the number 100. It seems most unlikely that a machine of this number would have been sold only a fortnight before ones bearing the numbers 299 and 300, which suggests that the existing Tabley hobby-horse is the one with the receipt dated 1st April 1819. If we have roughly an eight week gap between items 100 and 300, this in turn suggests that Johnson was manufacturing about 25 machines a week. This seems a reasonable enough figure, if we assume perhaps that he had a small team of workmen to assist him to meet the demand.

On this straight line basis the first machine would have been made at the beginning of March, but no doubt the manufacturing process was speeded up as both proficiency and demand increased, so that the earliest items could perhaps date from nearer the beginning of the year. As we know of no machine with a higher number than

---

[21] This item is at the Worthing Museum, who are unable to provide any provenance other than that the machine came to them in the 1930s from a Mr. R.E. Allard of Worthing.

Fig. 20. Denis Johnson velocipede no. 100. (photo courtesy of Glynn Stockdale). Found by Glynn Stockdale at Tabley House, where it can still be seen.

Fig. 21. Denis Johnson velocipede no. 100 (nose). Johnson machines were finished in a variety of colours. This is the only known surviving example painted yellow.

320, production may have largely ceased by about July or August 1819. It must however be emphasised that for the moment these suggested dates are mainly uncorroborated, and further evidence will need to be forthcoming before anything like a reliable chronology can be established. In particular, it should be borne in mind that the quoted dates of payment/receipt may not be equally related to the respective dates of manufacture/delivery.

Johnson numbered his machines by marking the Roman numerals on the top of the beam or backbone underneath the saddle, sometimes also on the underside of the wooden saddle itself, and on at least one occasion on the armrest or balance-board. The Nijmegen example (see Fig. 22) is of the underside of the restored saddle upholstery, with the all important (and late) number CCCXVI (316) now framed in a leather window.

The patent specification contains one puzzle. The drawings show the steering of the machine to be by way of a handle and light curved bar to "the axis, or axis carriage of the front wheel" as Johnson describes it. In fact, this early arrangement had by the June 1819 date of the specification to some extent given way to the more indirect steering shown in the drawing *Jack mounted on his Dandy Charger* (see Fig. 23), which is dated 1st March 1819 (the joke is a play on the term 'dandy charger', which the artist takes to mean a machine for charging dandies – instead of a machine on which dandies charge).

Fig. 22. Denis Johnson velocipede no. 316 (photo courtesy of 'Velorama', the National Bicycle Museum of The Netherlands, Nijmegen). The underside of the restored saddle displaying the late number CCCXVI.

Dashing Dandies

Fig. 23. 'Jack Mounted on his Dandy Charger' (1819 print, author's collection). The sailor's claim to be doing "ten knots an hour" (about 11½ m.p.h.) seems somewhat excessive – eight or at the most ten miles per hour was probably about the maximum on level ground.

32

Fig. 24. Denis Johnson velocipede no. 221 (photo courtesy of Copenhagen City Museum). This machine has apparently been at the Copenhagen City Museum (or in its store) since its inception in 1901.

According to John Fairburn, it was "drawn by an eminent Artist, from one of the latest improvements of the Machine".

One might have expected Johnson to have referred to the later arrangement in his patent specification, at least as an alternative. The fact that he did not do so suggests that, although he certainly incorporated direct steering in his machines, he did not claim to have originated this important improvement.

The wooden handle to which the metal steering bar was attached was again of two different types. The more common one (to judge from the surviving examples) was straight and comprised a square central section with rounded hand grips at either end.[22] A less common version[23] was attractively curved and lacked the bulbous hand grips.

---

[22] See for example the illustrated Science Museum machine.
[23] See for example the illustrated Copenhagen and Tabley House machines.

Dashing Dandies

Fig. 25. Hobby-horse (photo courtesy of Canada Science & Technology Museum). Another machine that has found its way abroad. Although in the photo the rear wheel looks larger than the front one, they are in fact both said to be 27½" diameter.

A letter from the then Duke of Argyll dated 14th July 1941 throws further light on the family's Johnson-type machine. He says it was certainly used by the 6th Duke (1768-1839) and by his brother the 7th Duke (1777 to 1847). In some old memoirs the 6th Duke "is mentioned as racing for bets with people like the Duke of Hamilton and the Duke of Montrose in Hyde Park or at Brighton, where he was always going in the Prince Regent's time". It was apparently acquired at the Roseneath Castle sale, and eventually made its way to Canada (see Fig. 25).

The hobby-horse was clearly favoured by the Scottish aristocracy. According to the Drumkilbo House website, young David Nairne (sometimes known as 'Drummie') was an early Scottish rider. George Kinloch wrote a letter dated 17th June 1819 stating: "The Drummie has been practising on a velocipede lately, but not with great success".

Fig. 26. Denis Johnson velocipede no. 25 (photo courtesy of the former Mark Hall Cycle Museum, Harlow).

Dashing Dandies

Fig. 27. Denis Johnson velocipede no. 25. Detail from the earliest known machine, showing the brass ornamentation on the 'nose' and dome.

Fig. 28. Denis Johnson velocipede no. 25. Detail showing footrests.

Fig. 29. Denis Johnson velocipede no. 31 (private owner). Whilst the 'indirect' steering is the most significant feature, the machine also displays the single 'V' rear support bar to the arm rest.

Fig. 30. Denis Johnson velocipede no. 31 (private owner). The close up of the front wheel hub and boss shows what may originally have been footrests, now however fixed flush to the front fork.

The earliest known Johnson machine is number 25 (XXV), formerly at the Mark Hall Cycle Museum in Harlow. As can be seen from the photo illustration, this already incorporates the "improved" i.e. direct steering (see Fig. 26). The next earliest example is number 31 (XXXI) (the number was prior to restoration on the armrest – the original has been retained – as well as underneath the saddle and on the main beam). This is the only known surviving Johnson machine with the original 'indirect' steering, and hence an item of particular interest. As the photo illustration shows, it is very similar to the patent specification drawings – even to the extent of being painted green[24].

[24] A portion of the main beam had to be replaced during restoration – part of it has been retained with the machine and displays the same colour, as does the saddle cover.

Fig. 31. Hobby-horse (Ipswich Museum). An interesting machine with 'indirect' steering by an unknown maker. The saddle, saddle spring, chest rest and bar may be later modifications.

As the original steering arrangement is featured in a number of hobby-horse prints dating from March and April 1819[25], it would seem that for some while both types of machine were being made. One of only a few surviving pedestrian hobby-horses with steering by a long curved bar to the front wheel hub, is the one at the Ipswich Museum's store shown in the photo illustration. Unlike the Johnson original, the curved steering bar is supported and pivots at the top just in front of a relatively wide handlebar. This was a

---

[25] The illustrated *Johnson's Pedestrian Hobbyhorse Riding School*, the original of which dates from 10th March 1819, depicts only indirect steering machines.

sensible modification, as the curved bar of the Johnson machine would fall forward onto the ground when not in use, to judge from the surviving example.

Another occasional modification not shown in Johnson's patent drawings was the addition of projections on either side at the base of the front forks, to serve as footrests when a good speed had been achieved, no doubt particularly when going downhill. This small detail is of some importance in the history of the bicycle. Although von Drais must be given all credit for the invention of the two-wheeler, he did not in fact provide his machine with footrests. Johnson's incorporation of this item underlines his confidence in the notion that it is entirely feasible to balance on two wheels, without relying on the rider's feet as supplementary supports.

The early former Mark Hall machine by Johnson has small rests attached to the front forks just above the axle, and as these are also a feature of the Science Museum's gentleman's hobby-horse they were presumably a common if not a standard fitting[26]. A fine machine, possibly built in the 1820s for the young 13th Earl of Eglinton and now owned by the National Museums of Scotland, is also fitted with footrests (see Fig. 32).

The only contemporary illustration of this useful accessory known to the author is in the illustrated print *Every Man on his Perch, or Going to Hobby Fair* (Fig. 18), in which three of the twenty-four machines are shown apparently fitted with such a device. The small drawing of a dandy on his hobby clearly shows two long curved struts rising from the bottom of the front forks, with the actual foot-rests somewhat above the level of the front wheel. The individual riding a machine in the right foreground of *Johnson's Pedestrian Hobbyhorse Riding School* print (see Fig. 33) would appear to be using footrests.

---

[26] The two Alnwick Castle machines, and the Pitt Rivers Museum one, both have holes for footrests but no such accessory.

Hobby-horses by Johnson and others

Fig. 32. Hobby-horse (photo © The Trustees of The National Museums of Scotland 1997). The suggestion has been made that the metal saddle bar might originally have been suspended within the spring, and that as there were both front and rear fork adjustments the original saddle would not itself need to have been height adjustable.

41

Dashing Dandies

Fig. 33. 'Johnson's Pedestrian Hobbyhorse Riding School' (1819 print, kind permission of Coventry Transport Museum). Probably the best known of all the hobby-horse prints. There are a number of references to it in this book.

42

A further reference to the hobby-horse in Scotland appears in the *Caledonian Mercury* (Edinburgh) for 14th June 1819. "Last week a dandy charger, or velocipede, ran off with its rider on Leith Walk, and coming violently in contact with a basket of eggs, overturned the rider, and sent him, with the contents of the basket, a rolling on the causeway. Upon recovering himself, the rider, to escape the fury of the egg woman, threw her a few shillings, remounted his charger, and galloped off".

A rare and late reference to the hobby-horse in Wales appears in the *Bristol Mercury* for 7th June 1819. "On Wednesday, a young gentleman, mounted on a Velocipede, commenced running with the Mail-Coach at the apex of the hill leading from Bangor-Ferry to Bangor, and succeeded in reaching the bottom of the hill before the Mail overtook him. We believe this is the first vehicle of the kind that has made its appearance in the Principality".

There is an interesting hybrid hobby-horse at Snowshill Manor in Worcestershire (see Fig. 34). For the most part it is quite a close copy of a Denis Johnson machine, save that the front wheel (30½") is larger than the rear wheel (26½"). The main beam has a much longer than usual 'nose', attached to which are footrests of the type commonly fitted to 'boneshaker' bicycles of the circa 1870 period. In the author's opinion, the machine clearly shows the influence of 'boneshaker' technology and probably dates from the later period. It was acquired by Charles Wade, the architect owner of Snowshill Manor, in August 1935.

A fascinating non-Johnson machine with an unusual steering handle, combined armrest and carrying box, a deeply curving frame with fixed saddle, and small footrests, could until recently be seen at the now closed Museum of Historic Cycling, Camelford, Cornwall, the former owners of which kindly supplied the modern photo illustration (Fig. 35). What would appear to be the same or a similar item (there are a number of modern copies), is also shown in the

Fig. 34. Hobby-horse copy (Snowshill Manor). An attractive item, but probably a late Nineteenth century version of the original Johnson machine.

Fig. 35. Hobby-horse (former Museum of Historic Cycling, Camelford). An unusual machine by an unknown maker. Compare fig. 36. A number of modern copies have been produced.

Fig. 36. Hobby-horse (19th century photo from 'The Hub' magazine). Compare fig. 35.

Fig. 37. Hobby-horse copy (photo courtesy of Ulster Folk and Transport Museum, Belfast). An excellent early replica of one of the two Johnson velocipedes still belonging to the Duke of Northumberland.

illustrated photo from *The Hub*[27] where it is described as 'Dandy and Hobby Horse, about 1819'. The photo (with three others) was taken for the magazine, but the machine itself may date from the hobby-horse era.

Another early copy is at the Ulster Folk & Transport Museum, on long term loan from the Science Museum (see Fig. 37). We know a certain amount about the origins of this machine. A letter dated 20th May 1904 to the Estates Office at Alnwick Castle from the Victoria & Albert Museum refers to: "the Hobby Horse which his Grace the Duke of Northumberland has been so good as to have

---

[27] 20th February 1897.

Fig. 38. Hobby-horse (St. John's Museum, Warwick, photo courtesy of Bill Haylor). Another recently discovered good quality Johnson-type machine by an unknown maker. Particular features are the deeply curved frame, saddle spring and footrests. The steering bar is facing the wrong way.

prepared for this Museum". It is an accurate copy of the larger of the two machines still at Alnwick Castle, albeit that the wheels are slightly smaller[28]. The photo also displays the steering column the wrong way round.

An interesting and important machine has been found by Bill Haylor in the St. John's Museum, Warwick (Fig. 38). The broad configuration follows Johnson, but it has a saddle spring and other features which mark it out as by another maker.

---

[28] The photo also displays the steering column the wrong way round.

Denis Johnson's original name for the machine was 'Pedestrian Curricle'. A curricle was – and is – a two-wheeled open carriage drawn by two side-by-side horses. It features in a short poem 'The Whip Club'[29]:

> What can *Men of Fashion* do?
> Why, drive a *Curricle and two*.
> Can Men of Fashion do no more?
> Yes, drive a smart *Barouche and four*.
> Do Men of Fashion end with this?
> May they not *drive too fast?* – Oh yes!

In fact, Johnson's 'Pedestrian Curricle' name was seldom if ever used by anyone except him. Indeed, by the beginning of April 1819 Johnson himself was referring to the invention as a 'Pedestrian Machine'[30], though he did also describe it as a 'Velocipede, or Patent Curricle' in a May 1819 advert (see below). However, Johnson still considered 'Pedestrian Curricle' to be the machines "proper name", and said the popular alternatives such as 'dandy horse' were "ludicrous"[31]. An early term generally employed was 'Pedestrian Hobby-Horse' (or 'Hobbyhorse', 'Hobby Horse' or 'Hobby'). It is not known who first applied the 'hobby-horse' epithet, but it was an obvious enough term to describe a machine which could be seen as distantly related to the ancient stick-between-the-legs child's toy of the same name.

If 'Hobby-Horse' was perhaps the most popular name used to describe the English version of the invention, there really was no standard term. There were a wide variety of other descriptions, including 'Pedestrian Carriage', 'Walking Accelerator', 'Swift Walker', 'Wooden Horse', 'German Horse', 'French Hobby-Horse' and 'Irish Jaunting Car'. Another popular name was 'Dandy-Charger' (or 'Dandy-Horse' or 'Dandy Hobby'), referring to the

---

[29] Published in the *Sporting Magazine* for June 1809.
[30] Receipt with Tabley papers, John Rylands Library.
[31] Adverts in Bristol and Bath newspapers in April 1819.

foppish individuals who often rode the machines. The fact that this came later than the 'hobby-horse' epithet is confirmed in the *Bath Chronicle* for 9th April 1819: "The new hobby-horse machines have been nick-named *dandy chargers*".

But in many instances newspapers and periodicals referred more respectfully to the hobby-horse by the French word 'Velocipede', possibly coined by von Drais (or originating in Italy).

It is perhaps worth highlighting the distinction between the term 'hobby-horse' (or its variations) and 'velocipede'. Both words were used synonymously to describe Johnson's machine in England in 1819. However, the essence of the 'hobby-horse' was that it was propelled by pushing with the feet on the ground (which usually meant that it only had two wheels). The word 'velocipede' soon came to have a wider use in this country, covering all types of rider-propelled machines, including those with three or four wheels often driven by some form of treadle mechanism. It continued to be used as the main generic term for some fifty years, when it was largely superseded by the words 'bicycle', 'tricycle' and related terms.

But to return to our story. Having obtained his patent three days before Christmas 1818, we can perhaps reasonably assume that Denis Johnson began manufacturing the new machine in earnest during January 1819. The *Monthly Magazine* for 1st March 1819 has a lengthy article on 'Mr Johnson's Velocipede, or Swift Walker', which concludes: "It is exhibited daily; and, *although never made public* [author's italics] has been already viewed by many thousands, many of whom have exercised, and all have approved, it".

This appears to have been a clever marketing strategy, that is, to whet the public appetite before actually selling the machine on the open market (or perhaps Johnson was simply waiting until he had built up sufficient stock to meet the anticipated demand). Fairburn's booklet is undated but contains the following passage:

Mr. Johnson's Repository is daily thronged with visitors, and it is amusing to see his servant riding about a long room to show the Horse, threading the carriages, and wheeling and turning with great precision. They may also be seen in a large Exhibition-room, near Exeter-Change, Strand; and at another in Brewer-Street, Golden-square; which have been engaged for that purpose.

Despite the statement in the *Monthly Magazine,* the likelihood is perhaps that the item was first publicly sold some time during February – both the *Gentleman's Magazine* and the *Sporting Magazine* for March 1819 refer to it as being "already in general use".

It was probably at or about this time that a certain R. Childs devised "An economical plan for examining the merits of the Velocipede, or Swift Walker, and a chance of obtaining one for five shillings". He explained his scheme in his own handwriting on the left hand side of a large piece of paper,[32] at the head of which was an illustration of a man on a hobby-horse beneath the somewhat hackneyed Shakespearian quotation "A horse, a horse, my kingdom for a horse". This was the velocipede plan:

> Forty persons subscribing five shillings each, will raise a sum sufficient to purchase one and pay the expenses of carriage &c attending it. After the subscribers have investigated the principle of the machine it is proposed to dispose of it by lottery, and whoever shall be so fortunate to draw the ticket, marked *prize*, will be owner of a horse that will eat neither hay nor corn, for the small sum above-named.
>
> N.B. The Lottery to be drawn at the Fleece Inn.
>
> Money to be paid at the time of Subscribing.
>
> R. Childs.

The right-hand side of the sheet was left clear for the names of forty subscribers who wished to take part in the sweepstake. One can

---

[32] Now at the Science Museum Library.

imagine the paper being perhaps left on the bar of the Fleece Inn[33]. Forty punters duly subscribed their names, and no doubt paid their stakes to the organizer. Against each name are three numbers, 11-7-12, 7-4-5, 9-5-8, and so on. In the case of the first few names a total is also shown i.e. 30, 16, 23 (someone couldn't count) etc. What the author surmises must have happened is that someone suggested it would be more fun if, instead of simply drawing a ticket, each participant had three throws of a set of two dice, the player with the highest total score winning the sweepstake and acquiring the velocipede. And as if to prove that fortune favours the brave – and the enterprising – the winner with a total score of 32 turned out to be none other than – Mr. R. Childs! One can imagine the comments of his friends and acquaintances.

It was it seems in March 1819 that Denis Johnson opened his riding schools at 377 Strand and 40 Brewer Street (Soho). The *Literary Gazette* for 27th February 1819 has an item on the 'Pedestrian Carriage, or Walking Accelerator' stating that "a riding school is about to be opened for them". The *Johnson's Pedestrian Hobbyhorse Riding School* print is (as previously stated) dated 10th March 1819, and makes reference to both addresses. An advert by Johnson in the *Morning Chronicle* for 12th April 1819 refers to the machine being available for inspection at an address near Cheapside and at 40 Brewer Street, Golden Square.

---

[33] Presumably a London tavern – the name was a popular one, no less than a dozen being listed in Foster's circa 1900 *Inns, Taverns, Alehouses, Coffee Houses, etc. in and around London*.

Chapter 4

Johnson, son of Johnson

But Johnson did not confine his activities to London. It would appear that he commissioned his son (almost certainly his illegitimate son, John Johnson, as no other son is known) to tour England to exhibit the machine and provide riding instructions – and no doubt to take purchase orders. Although no Christian name is provided, the illustrated print Johnson, the *First Rider on the Pedestrian Hobbyhorse* (Fig. 39), clearly relates to this individual and not his father.

The tour started in Bristol in mid-April, and moved on from there to Bath. An advert in the *Bath & Cheltenham Gazette* refers to the proposed exhibition "by MR. JOHNSON, the Son of the Patentee and Constructor of the useful and interesting Invention, who has acquired extraordinary celebrity by his London exhibition and displays in his riding the velocity and graceful evolutions which it is capable of".[34] Johnson Junior then moved on to Manchester and Leeds.

The story continues in *Aris's Birmingham Gazette*[35]:

> VELOCIPEDE, OR PATENT CURRICLE. MR JOHNSON takes the Liberty of announcing to the Gentry and Inhabitants of Birmingham, that he will display before them the various Revolutions and Changes of Motion which are capable of being shown on this truly unique Vehicle, at the Stork Hotel, Square, Birmingham.

---

[34] 21st April 1819.
[35] 10th May 1819.

Fig. 39. 'Johnson, the First Rider on the Pedestrian Hobbyhorse' (1819 print, author's collection). A contemporary Bath newspaper refers to Mr Johnson's "unparalleled display of skill, grace and elegance" on his velocipede, and of the capability of the machine "being guided with that precision when at full speed, as for both wheels to pass over a sixpence casually thrown upon the ground".

> Admission, 1.s each – Youths, 6d. N.B. Six Lessons is sufficient to perfect any one –
>
> Hours of Exhibition from Ten till Seven.

By the end of the month Johnson's son was in Liverpool. The *Liverpool Mercury*[36] speaks of "the performance of Mr. JOHNSON, who exhibits at the Music-hall", referring to "the graceful movements of which (the velocipede) is capable in skilful hands ... as performed by the gentleman we have mentioned". The same issue of the newspaper tells us that elsewhere in the city a less graceful performance has taken place:

> On Tuesday evening, while a gentleman was exercising on one of the Velocipedes at the Assembly-room in Cook-street, he was *thrown* with such force from his seat that he had three of his teeth knocked out by the fall. – It is added that notwithstanding this unpleasant accident, the gentleman means to persevere *"in spite of his teeth".*

The merits of the velocipede were again being exhibited in Liverpool at the beginning of July. It seems that later the same month Denis Johnson himself had arrived in America, an unidentified New York paper being quoted as saying that "the constructor himself" had "imported himself by the last arrival from London, in order to supply the market".

Clearly our hero (supported by his son) was no slouch when it came to promoting his product.

No business accounts are known to survive, but the suggestion has been made that Johnson must have done well financially from selling his machines (quite apart from his other related activities). "The first cost of the machine to the patentee was not more than forty or fifty shillings [£2-£2.50]; but the price to the public is from

---

[36] 28th May 1819.

eight to ten pounds"[37]. There is no doubt that large numbers were seen at the height of the craze, but the only reliable guide we have is the actual numbering on existing Johnson machines, the highest currently known being as previously stated 320.

If we take an average sale price of £9.00 and an average manufacturing cost of £2.25 in today's terms (based on the quoted figures), and assume conservatively a sale of only 320 machines, the net profit would have been £2,160, a quite substantial sum in 1819 – perhaps in the region of £125,000 today.

There is no indication that Johnson reduced the price of his machines after they had been on the market for a few months. In February 1819 the poet John Keats wrote to relatives referring to the Velocipede as "the nothing of the day", adding that "a handsome gelding will come to eight guineas, however they will soon be cheaper, unless the army takes to them"[38]. Nevertheless, the Duke of Northumberland paid £22 for two machines as late as the end of May 1819.

But it is possible that Denis Johnson may not in fact have made quite the 'killing' which these figures indicate. An item in *Aris's Birmingham Gazette*[39] refers to Johnson as the patentee, threatens legal proceedings if the patent is breached, and states that the machine is exhibiting at 377 Strand "where orders for the same will be taken and executed accordingly".

Yet at the end of the same week we find a notice in substantially the same form, but with one vital difference. This reads:

> THE PEDESTRIAN CARRIAGE OR MACHINE
>
> For promoting Health, diminishing the Labour of Persons in Walking, and enabling them to Travel with greater ease and celerity.

---

[37] *La Belle Assemblée* for May 1819.
[38] *Collected Letters*, as quoted by Jeanne Mackenzie in her 1981 *Cycling* anthology.
[39] Monday 22nd March 1819.

> His Majesty, by Letters Patent of the last year (1818), having granted to Mr. DENNIS JOHNSON, the Patentee of the invention), the sole licence and authority to make and vend the above Patent Machine, and Mr. Johnson having assigned all his right and interest therein to S. MERSEY, of Long Acre, London, Notice is hereby given to all persons that in case they shall in any way or manner infringe on the said letters patent, by making or selling such Carriage or Machine or any Machine in imitation thereof, they will, on discovery, be immediately proceeded against either at law or in equity, as shall be thought most adviseable.
>
> The public are respectfully informed, that the above machine is now exhibiting at No. 377, in the Strand, London, opposite to Mr. Ackerman's Repository, and that all orders for the same, directed to Mr. Mercey, No. 71, Long Acre, London, (the Assignee of the patent), will be duly attended to and executed accordingly. The price for the Machine Eight Guineas.[40]

Where did all this leave the entrepreneurial Denis Johnson? Samuel Merscy (apparently the correct spelling) was a 'laceman', not a coachmaker. He had obtained a patent (no.4156 of 1817) for an improved method of weaving livery and coach lace. No doubt he had premises amongst the "great colony of coachmakers" of Long Acre in order to supply coach lace and livery lace for coachmen. Exactly how he fits into the hobby-horse story is not clear. On the face of it, the notice suggests that Merscy had become the absolute owner of Johnson's patent and business.

But despite the fact that as assignee of the patent Merscy requested all orders be sent to him at 71 Long Acre, the evidence of the London trade directories is that, throughout the period of manufacture of the machine, Samuel Merscy remained a laceman and Denis

---

[40] Inserted in the *Norfolk Chronicle and Norwich Gazette* for Saturday 27th March 1819 (as well as in other newspapers).

Johnson remained a coachmaker. And of course we hear more of Johnson after March 1819, but nothing of Merscy[41].

Possibly further research will throw more light on the business relationship of the two individuals. In the meantime, the author's tentative conclusion is that Merscy may have acquired Johnson's patent for a sum which Johnson used as working capital to finance his expanding hobby-horse manufactory. Merscy may at the same time have granted Johnson a licence to continue to make and sell machines, on payment of a royalty for each item sold. It may have been agreed that orders for machines would be directed to Number 71 but executed at Number 75, so that Merscy could keep a check on the position. However, at the moment all this can only be a working hypothesis.

But to return to the substance of the notice. The fact that it was thought necessary to issue a strongly-worded warning against infringement of the Johnson patent in a number of newspapers, suggests that there had already by March 1819 been perhaps fairly widespread unauthorised copying. No doubt some of these copies were simplified versions produced by local craftsmen on a one-off basis.

A clear infringement of the Johnson patent occurred in Liverpool. Three issues of the *Liverpool Mercury* tell the story. On 2nd April 1819 we read that a velocipede "has been manufactured in this town" from the description in the *Mercury*. On 21st May, when Johnson's son was exhibiting his father's machine in Liverpool, an item appeared under the heading 'Caution. The Genuine Patent Velocipede.' The patentee wanted to "assure the Public, that the Velocipedes now in this town are spurious imitations of the patent ones; and that the exhibitors are very imperfectly skilled in manoeuvring them.

---

[41] For example, Johnson inserted an advert referring to the appointment of Hugh Black as his Leeds agent towards the end of April 1819, with no reference to Merscy.

Mr. Johnson is now in Liverpool, for the express purpose of exhibiting it in its true character". On 4th June we read that "various attempts of evasive makers" had "infringed on the interest of the Patent" and that any such infringement would result in action being taken.

As early as the beginning of February 1819 we learn that: "On Monday last, was exhibited at Swaffham, one of the new invented walking machines, or Accelerators, made of iron by Mr. Drake Youngs, an ingenious blacksmith at Castleacre"[42]. Bearing in mind that Johnson only obtained his patent on 22nd December 1818 (and that the specification and drawings were only filed six months later), the Norfolk blacksmith can have lost no time in producing his version of the machine – presumably without applying to the patentee for permission to do so. Another largely iron machine can be seen in the Mossman Collection at the Stockwood Park Museum, Luton (see Fig. 40).

It is interesting to read that these early copies were made of iron, as the Johnson patent specification does state: "The machine … consists of a beam made of wood *or metal* [author's italics] of sufficient strength to bear the weight of the person who is to ride it".

In an unpublished doctoral thesis *The Bicycle Era in American History*[43] Norman Dunham, speaking of the hobby-horse, states: "Riders soon noted a defect in construction, however. The first British vehicles, like the French, had been built almost entirely of wood, but when the damp island climate caused this to warp or crack, makers changed many parts to iron or steel". Only a Twentieth century American source is quoted in support, and the present author is sceptical. There is no evidence to support the notion that Britain's "damp island climate "should within a very short time cause

---

[42] *Norwich Mercury*, 6th February 1819.
[43] Harvard University, 1957.

Fig. 40. Hobby-horse (Stockwood Park Museum, Luton). A unique machine made largely of iron.

machines "to warp or crack". The only major change in the Johnson velocipede was the early one from 'indirect' to 'direct' steering. And the only known all iron machines are the two referred to above.

Another Norfolk example (Fig. 41) can be seen at the Strangers' Hall Museum in Norwich, being said to date from around 1820. Like a number of other copies, the design is more primitive than the Johnson hobby-horse and lacks the forearm rest. However, it has two interesting features. Although essentially a wooden machine, the wheel rims (but not the spokes) are metal. The seat (the height of which is adjustable) is attached to a rudimentary metal spring.

Johnson machines found their way to distant parts of the realm, but there is some evidence of unauthorised commercial production by other makers. We have referred to the situation in Liverpool. The author suspects the following advert inserted in the *Salisbury*

Fig. 41. Hobby-horse (photo courtesy Strangers' Hall Museum, Norwich). A curious piece. The carved horse's head is reminiscent of the child's hobby-horse stick.

and Winchester Journal[44] by a Dorset maker is another unauthorised attempt to undercut the London manufacturer:

> VELOCIPEDES. THE Public are respectfully informed, they may be supplied with the newly invented machine, called a VELOCIPEDE, at various prices, from four to seven guineas, (according to the make and decorations), by John Rutter, of Shaftesbury, who will feel obliged by any orders he may be favoured with. One at four guineas constantly kept for inspection; and with which any individual may be accommodated, for a short time, at a reasonable charge.

Of course, it could be that John Rutter was simply a West Country agent for Johnson (or should we still be saying Merscy), but the

---

[44] 3rd May 1819.

low prices quoted – which would have had to include the agent's commission and transport from London – makes this seem unlikely. Another possibility is that Rutter obtained a licence from the patentee to make the machines himself, but again this seems unlikely as Johnson's own machines were being promoted on a nationwide basis.

Denis Johnson continued in business as a coachmaker at 75 Long Acre for a number of years after the pedestrian hobby-horse had been largely forgotten, initially on his own account. He is still to be found under his own name in the *Post Office London Directory* for 1824, but the following year the same directory refers to Johnson & Allen, Coach-makers, 75 Long Acre (with no individual coach-maker of either name being listed). Denis Johnson's partner was another coachmaker, John Allen, who also became his son-in-law as a result of marrying Denis's older daughter Mary.

The partnership between the two men continued for about nine years, until Johnson's death aged 73 years on Christmas Day, 1833. He was buried at St. Martin's Chapel, Camden Town, on 2nd January 1834. Denis Johnson's undated Will was proved in the Prerogative Court of Canterbury, London, on 24th March 1834. The Estate Duty Register[45] records that he left personal estate (including lease-hold) to the value of nearly a thousand pounds (£934.9.4), a fair sum by early Nineteenth century standards.

Johnson's handwritten Will[46] provides us with an insight into his character. He was clearly a methodical individual, giving precise instructions as to how his wishes were to be carried into effect. His executors (his two sons-in-law) were to have "the stock of all descriptions taken and minutely taken as if it were strangers coming in on purchase". He was careful with his money, and anxious to

---

[45] IR 26/1355 no.1101.
[46] National Archives reference PROB 10/5457 28681.

save "unnecessary expense" either in connection with his funeral or the administration of his estate. He was obviously proud of the business he had built up over the year "whatever I am possessed of has been gained by sheer Industry and Labour". He was anxious that it should not be adversely affected by the sudden withdrawal of his capital – the payment of gifts and legacies was to be "at the time most convenient for the business, I mean that money should not be drawn out of the business to check its progress".

But Johnson was not only a business man he was also a kindly man, making especially thoughtful provision for his sister, leaving her to the care of his two daughters "should she survive me and want that assistance that the aged require". He was also concerned for his younger daughter Ann: "in case that anything should happen that she my daughter Ann, which God forbid, should want a home, it is my will that she shall have a sitting room, a bedroom, a kitchen and servants room etc in this house".

Denis Johnson refers in his Will to his "dear wife" who predeceased him. Nevertheless, as previously stated, it appears he had a son born out of wedlock, John Johnson, to whom he left the sum of £100 by his Will[47].

As Johnson expressly requested in his Will, the firm name of Johnson & Allen remained unchanged for many years after Denis's demise. However, by 1840 the address had altered to 72 Long Acre. The 1851 Census return shows John Allen, age 63, his wife Mary, age 56, his sons John and Francis aged 19 and 16 years respectively, and two younger daughters Frances and Martha, as well as another family, living at the 72 Long Acre address. By 1853 John Allen (probably still the father but conceivably the elder son) was simply using his own name.

---

[47] The reference to illegitimacy comes in a sworn statement to the Probate Court by John Allen.

The next change had occurred by 1867, in which year *Kelly's Post Office London Trades Directory* shows "Allen, John and Francis, coach and harness makers, at 71 & 72 Long Acre". The two brothers appear to have worked hard and prospered, as by 1880 *Kelly* is referring to them as being at "27, 28 & 29 &117 Long Acre WC & 3 Davies Street Berkeley Square W". At this date both members of the firm were tricycle riders, and were it seems selling such machines as agents, according to a letter in *Bicycling News*.

In 1887 we find a first reference to Frank Allen (possibly a grandson of the original John Allen and great-grandson of Denis Johnson) carrying on the coachmaking business, now only at 27, 28 & 29 Long Acre. The last entry for Frank Allen is in the directory for 1908.

It would seem that the Long Acre coachmaking business originally founded by the redoubtable Denis Johnson, pedestrian hobby-horse patentee, manufacturer and seller, was kept in existence by the Allen branch of his family for a further three generations spanning some ninety years, until the early years of the Twentieth century.

Chapter 5

The hobby-horse scene in England

The invention soon became known in London, and many persons now present can, no doubt, remember, how quickly this novelty was adopted by the public. The equality and swiftness of the motion when compared with walking which it so much resembled, recommended velocipedes to many persons who disliked the trouble and expense of keeping a horse, and the rapidity which could be acquired bore some resemblance to skating. The novelty and ingenuity of the idea quickly brought this invention into common use: in the New Road they might be seen in great numbers running every fine evening especially near Finsbury Square, and the top of the Portland Road, where they were let out for hire by the hour. Rooms for practice were opened in various parts of the town, and several expert riders made it their business to exhibit them in the principal cities of England. I am acquainted with individuals who went with their velocipedes from twenty to thirty miles in a day on excursions into the country, and many young men were in the habit of riding sixty miles or more in the course of a week. It is easy to see how beneficial this exercise must have been to the health of the riders, who were generally inhabitants of cities, and often occupied during the day in sedentary pursuits connected with their business.

Thomas Davies's lecture 'On the Velocipede' from which this quotation is taken, was as stated earlier delivered in May 1837, enabling him to speak both with first-hand knowledge of his topic and with the benefit of historical perspective. It provides an excellent view of the scene in town and country during the heyday of the pedestrian hobby-horse. In view of the relatively primitive nature of the machine the distances regularly covered may seem surprising. But even more impressive is the account of a "very adroit velocipedean" who rode the 400-odd miles from London to Falkirk in Scotland, and later made a long excursion in France, on a "wooden horse"[48]. And it was from Pau, in Southern France, that an English engineer made a 300-odd mile journey over the Pyrenees to Madrid, apparently during the early part of 1820 – according to von Drais himself writing in a German fashion magazine[49].

An article on 'The Pedestrian Carriage' in *The Examiner*[50] concludes: "These owl-headed philosophers would look amazingly profound and contemptuous, if they heard us call this newly invented Wooden Horse an excellent discovery, and one of the many fresh instances of the progress of experimental philosophy. Yet such it is."

In his 1869 book *The Velocipede, its Past, its Present & its Future*, 'J.F.B.' (identified as J.F. Bottomley-Firth) tells us: "Clergymen used the new machine to visit their parishioners, and to travel between scattered parishes. Postmen with their letter bags sailing in the wind, rode the dandy-horse; young swells of the period used it, not only for exercise but for the purpose of making calls; and strangest if not saddest spectacle of all, old men who had hitherto borne blameless characters for sedateness and respectability, were to be seen careering along on the dandy-horse".

Although these substantially later comments by J.F.B. must be treated with some reserve, according to von Drais (writing in the German fashion magazine) the velocipede was indeed used in Britain for

---

[48] *Howitt's Visits to Remarkable Places* (vol. 2), 1841.
[49] *Journal für Literatur, Kunst, Luxus und Mode*, Weimar, July 1820.
[50] 11th April 1819.

the carrying of mail in 1820 (Fig. 42). The illustrated Sidebethem print *Hobby-horses jockying the Mail!!* shows a 'four-in-hand' team of riders pulling a Royal Mail coach in the open country, but in reality the machine would presumably have been employed by individual postmen around town.

Clearly much thought was given as to how to make practical employment of the machine. A novel use of it for measuring roads "by attaching the necessary index and machinery to the back part of it" was suggested by a correspondent in the *Nottingham Review* for 21st May 1819.

The legend below the illustrated print *Pedestrian Hobbyhorse* published by Rudolph Ackermann in February 1819 (see Fig. 43) described how to employ the new means of locomotion. "This Machine is of the most simple kind, supported by two light wheels running on the same line; the front wheel turning on a pivot, which, by means of a short lever, gives the direction in turning to one side or the other, the hind wheel always running in one direction".

"The rider mounts it, and seats himself in a saddle conveniently fixed on the back of the horse (if allowed to be called so), and placed in the middle between the wheels; the feet are placed flat on the ground, so that in the first step to give the Machine motion, the heel should be the part of the foot to touch the ground, and so on with the other foot alternately, as if walking on the heels, observing always to begin the movement very gently. In the front, before the rider, is placed a cushion to rest the arms on while the hands hold the lever which gives direction to the Machine, as also to balance if it inclining to the other side when the opposite arm is pressed on the cushion".

According to James T. Lightwood[51], an enterprising London shoe-maker "netted a pretty sum by manufacturing a shoe with iron sole

---

[51] In his 1928 book *The Romance of the Cyclists' Touring Club*

The hobby-horse scene in England

Fig. 42. "Hobby-horses jockying the Mail!" (1819 print, kind permission of Coventry Transport Museum.). The print is dedicated to the 'Four in hand Club'; the members of which are described in issues of the 'Sporting Magazine' for 1809 as "celebrated charioteers". The club was it seems in existence from 1808 to 1820.

Fig. 43. Pedestrian Hobbyhorse (1819 print, author's collection). The earliest known hobby-horse print. Although dated simply 'February 1819' it is featured as Fig. 9 in Ackermann's 'Repository of Arts' for 1st February 1819.

which greatly aided the rider in his velocipeding exercise". In the first issue of *Bicycling* (later *Cycling*) in August 1878 in an article 'Riders I have known', Mark Mitton tells us: "The very first rider I knew was a solid, good-hearted, self-denying, tradesman in Shropshire, who rode nearly half a century ago a fearfully and wonderfully constructed 'Dandy Horse' … I heard of his former exploits – how he had steel caps to his boot toes, and that even then these soon were thin with perpetually spurring mother earth". And a lengthy poem *Jonah Tink* by John Atkin[52] contains the following lines:

> A dandy youth he was, whose mien,
> Could scarcely for shirt neck be seen;
> With copper soles, and spurs of steel,
> Each boot plate upon the heel;
> That he might faster on proceed,
> He rode on a *velocipede*.

Whilst there is ample evidence that the pedestrian hobby-horse became the plaything of the Regency dandies, to the extent that the machine even became known in some quarters as the 'dandy-horse', its use was by no means confined to the London beaux. A check on a sample of regional newspapers suggests that the hobby-horse in its Johnsonian form was widely available throughout the country by about April 1819, confirming the statement by Thomas Davies on this point. We read for example in the *Norfolk Chronicle and Norwich Gazette* for 17th April 1819, under the heading Velocipedes, that "Several of these machines, denominated Pedestrian Hobby Horses, have been exhibiting here this week" i.e. presumably Norwich, where the paper was published. On the same day the *Norwich Mercury* contained an advertisement for the machine:

> PANTHEON, RANELAGH GARDENS. THE Nobility, Gentry, and Public are very respectfully informed, that FINCH has procured an ACCELERATOR, or WALKING PERAMBULATOR, which

---

[52] Published Newark, 1823.

will be opened for inspection on Monday next. In order more fully to satisfy the minds of such Gentlemen as may choose to honour it with their approbation, he has engaged a young man to instruct them in its use, as it appears there is some difficulty in their first management, as well as a liability to damage.

It will most necessarily require some regulation, for the convenience of all, which must of course be produced by a series of rules, which he will have the honour of submitting for the Public's approbation. To digress upon the qualities of this ingenious and portable machine, would carry more explanation with it than Finch is capable of performing towards it; but takes leave to observe, should the taste and inclination of Gentlemen be directed towards it, he will provide, for their comfort and entertainment, ANOTHER.

Just two days later we read in the Lewes column of the *Sussex Weekly Advertiser* that "The Dandy's Hobby's was exercised here on Saturday, and underwent the discipline of many *rough riders*". The following week the same newspaper reported that: "The Dandy Horse, stated in our last to be under exercise here, soon broke down, so that there appears, in this species of horse-dealing even, to be *Jockeyship*; but quaere, was this Hobby *warranted sound* to the purchaser?" The week after this the paper carried a short verse:

> On seeing the Dandy Hobbies at Lewes
>
> Astride a *Broom* in days of old,
> Wizards and Witches, as we're told,
> Skim'd thro' the air so quick;
> But *Dandies* in the present day
> (No *Conjurors* in truth are they)
> Bestride the simple *Stick*!

The hobby-horse had arrived in Nottingham by the end of April 1819[53], and a speedy twenty-eight mile ride by two young men is

---

[53] *Nottingham Review*, 30th April 1819.

recorded there two months later[54]. At the beginning of May, a Leicester individual advertised that he had obtained a 'VELOCIPEDE, Or, Ambulant Adjutor' available for inspection or use[55].

The extent of interest in the new machine is clear when we read that: "There was an attempted exhibition of three of the Velocipedes, on Sunday, in Hyde Park; but they were so impeded in their operations by the curiosity of the promenaders, that after getting about half way along the King's private road, towards Kensington Gardens, they suddenly turned about, and retired by the gate at Hyde Park-corner, amidst the shouts of some two or three dozen lads, who seemed disposed to persecute them with still more serious annoyance"[56]. The previous week the same newspaper had reported: "A gentleman, mounted upon his wooden hobby-horse, on the Camberwell-road, on Monday, attracted a great crowd, from the pressure of which he was, at his earnest solicitation, extricated by a passing stage-coachman, who carried him and his horse off on the roof".

According to Mrs Alec Tweedie in *Hyde Park, its History and Romance*[57], "practically every surviving method of locomotion has heralded its earliest votaries within the precincts of the Park, where the foot-propelled "hobby-horse" proved the forerunner of the bicycle". Mrs Tweedie later states the machine "was almost a peculiarity of Hyde Park, where the young beaux of the middle-nineteenth century disported themselves on the bone-racking contrivance, for few ventured out into the streets or to the open country upon it". The reference should of course have been to the early nineteenth century, and there are numerous examples of much wider use of the machine than the authoress suggests. However, the contemporary author Fairburn does comment: "If we are *literally* to shoot folly as

---

[54] *Nottingham Review*, 25th June 1819.
[55] *Leicester Journal*, 7th May 1819.
[56] *Birmingham Commercial Herald*, 3rd April 1819.
[57] London, 1908.

Dashing Dandies

Fig. 44. 'Perambulators in Hyde Park' (1819 print, courtesy of Lewis Walpole Library). The narrative below the print acknowledges Baron von Drais as the inventor, and refers to the action as "similar to the motion used in Skaiting" (as referred to in Chapter 1).

it flies, Hyde Park, on a Sunday would be strewed with dead, and not a Dandy left to tell the tale". And one of the many 1819 prints depicting the hobby-horse in use is the illustrated *Perambulators in Hyde Park!*

The novel item was such a newsworthy phenomenon that, like the modern 'UFO', reports of its appearance were not always to be relied on. Under the heading *The Velocipede or Wooden Horse* in the *Sussex Weekly Advertiser*[58] we read:

> This hobby having excited much public curiosity, it was, as we are informed, on Wednesday evening given out at Worthing, that it would, on the following morning, be exhibited in all its paces, at one of the Libraries; a great number of the amateurs of novelty, and others, in consequence assembled in the South-street, to witness the movements of this mechanical *prodigy*; but after buzzing and bustling about for a considerable time without seeing any preparation made for the wonderful performance, they at length found out –
>
> That 'twas *April Fool Day!* – So they all slipt away,
>
> Abashed at their credulity, but not offended with the worthy Librarian, who had no hand in the *hoax*, and has intimated his intention of yet gratifying the curiosity of his friends, by getting a hobby from town for that purpose".

Coincidentally, on the same day a somewhat similar event took place further west. One cannot help thinking that it would make a fine silent movie clip:

> A HOAX. On Thursday morning last a placard was posted up in one of the principal shops in Blandford, stating that a bid of 50 guineas was depending between one of the new-invented *Hobby Horses* and the Mail Coach, which should arrive first at the Crown Inn. Accordingly, about half an hour before the arrival of

---

[58] 5th April 1819.

the Mail, the road between Blandford and Pimperne was thronged with spectators to see this new-invented mode of travelling; but on the arrival of the Mail, it was discovered to be a hoax, – as a boy appeared with a pole, having a card affixed with the words "This is the first of April".[59]

There must have been an impish essence in the English air on Thursday, 1st April 1819. A poem 'The Velocipede'[60] which was somewhat reminiscent of Browning's 'The Pied Piper of Hamelin', tells the metropolitan story so vividly that it seems worth quoting at length:

> By hand-bills it was publicly made known
> That some high-mettled hobby would be shown,
> On Thursday afternoon at half-past three,
> By that fam'd jockey, called the patentee;
> Who would display its most surprising power;
> And ride on foot twelve hundred poles an hour.

The "fam'd jockey" would in fact have been Johnson junior, not his father the patentee. The old 'rod, pole or perch' measurement was equivalent to 5½ yards, so the claimed riding speed of 1,200 poles an hour was only 3¾ miles an hour. No doubt Johnson junior could in fact have done much better than this. The poem continues:

> The bait was laid: – not sooner laid than taken;
> Some shops were clos'd and many more forsaken;
> Some took two hours to put themselves in state,
> Some could not dine for fear of being late;
> Some crept, some walk'd, some ran with all their speed,
> To see this wonder, call'd Velocipede.
> Soon from Wake Green to Smithfield market-place
> The windows were replete with "magic grace";
> The road was all confusion, life, and noise,
> And ev'ry tree a rookery of boys.

---

[59] *Salisbury and Winchester Journal,* 5th April 1819.
[60] Published in full in the *Birmingham Commercial Herald* for 10th April 1819.

Indeed, some time before the clock struck two
The streets were swarming with a motley crew,
Of ev'ry shape and colour, sex and size,
Profession and description, save the wise:
Foot men in companies, and horse in troops,
And smirking belles in formidable groups;
Old men with crutches, and old men with staves,
Monkeys and mountebanks, and other knaves;
Mechanics, farmers, and a specious show

Of dandies: – ten or twenty in a row;
Whose heads were blocks of most prodigious size,
And whisker'd from the ARM-PITS to the eyes.
These things were bound and bandag'd , neck and waist,
With steel and whalebone, buckram, starch, and paste;
So uniform their motions and their features,
They looked like wax-work more than living creatures.

Those, with the rest, stood still or stalk'd about
In great suspense, though no one seem'd to doubt:
They waited long; the go-cart did not come;
Some few, at length reluctantly went home.
At five o'clock some one was heard to say –
"Why, – it's the First of April! – All fools' day!"

It was enough. The final blow was struck.
It circulated like th' electric shock.
A shock it was to all the gaping crowd;
Though whisper'd low, their feelings spoke aloud:
They slunk away, as from a dirty action,
Fill'd with chagrin and sore dissatisfaction;
And evr'y one was ready, for a wonder,
To blame himself for making such a blunder.

Chapter 6

Matches against time, racing, accidents and prosecutions

In the late Eighteenth and early Nineteenth centuries wagers and 'matches against time' were very much in vogue and provided great interest. One of the most famous involved the pedestrian feat of a certain Captain Barclay, who undertook in 1809 to walk a mile every hour for a thousand consecutive hours. He succeeded and won a bet of 1,000 guineas.[61] It was to be expected therefore that when the hobby-horse appeared on the scene there would be similar challenges.

As early as 17th March 1819 we read in the *Bury and Norwich Post* that "A Military Gentleman has made a bet to go to London by the side of the coach", and the same month the *European Magazine* records that "the Accelerator has even beat the Brighton four horse coach by half an hour". Exactly a month after the Bury and *Norwich Post* report, we hear in the *Norwich Mercury* of a "person from the country" who "exhibited upon the Castle Hill, an Accelerator, or Wooden Horse, with which he appeared to travel at a considerable rate". This individual "offered to make a bet that he would travel to London in 14 hours by the help of the machine".

Another hobby-horse 'match against time' to go from Oxford to Woodstock (about eight miles) in an hour was arranged by three

---

[61] *Sporting Magazine*, July 1809

individuals, who "performed a reel in the Great Room, Cross Keys, Queen Street, in a style which delighted every one present"[62].

Further south, we learn that: "THURSDAY, April 15, a lad of the name of Wilds. of Canterbury, undertook for a considerable wager, to ride a *velocipede*, or dandy charger, from Upstreet to Canterbury, a distance of six miles, within an hour, which he accomplished with apparent ease, nine minutes and a half within time"[63]. Other reports tell us "he was accompanied by some persons in gigs and on horseback" (also giving the youth's name as Wild, not Wilds).

But the previous month an even faster time had been achieved. "A curious wager was decided on Saturday at Chigwell-row, between two gentlemen of Chinkford [presumably Chingford, Essex] named Brown and Jones for 25 gs. which went the greatest distance in one hour, each mounted on his 2-wheel hobby, which was determined in favour of Mr. Brown, who did nearly eight miles, beating his antagonist a quarter of a mile"[64].

A surely yet more impressive feat was performed later in the year. "AN extraordinary bet of 50 guineas has been decided by two gentlemen of St. Columb, Cornwall, one of whom undertook to run a velocipede from that place to Liskeard, a distance of 26 miles, in four hours. Notwithstanding the badness of the road, which caused the machine to move very heavily, he won his wager, by performing the journey twenty-one minutes within the time, with perfect ease"[65]. An average speed of just over seven miles an hour.

Apart from these 'matches against time', there seems to have been a limited amount of 'official' racing involving the hobby-horse. One of the earliest prints, the illustrated *Modern Olympics*[66] (see Fig. 45),

---

[62] *Oxford University and City Herald*, 17th April 1819.
[63] *Sporting Magazine*, April 1819.
[64] *Simpson's Salisbury Gazette*, 25th March 1819.
[65] *Sporting Magazine*, September 1819.
[66] Published 23rd February 1819.

Dashing Dandies

Fig. 45. 'Modern Olympics' (1819 print, author's collection). The reference in the title is to the ancient Greek Olympian Games, as the modern Olympic Games were only inaugurated in 1896.

78

shows dandies racing on the new velocipede. This print is also featured on the cover of this book. Another illustrated print, *Modern Pegasus or Dandy Hobbies in Full Speed*[67] (see Fig. 46), published 24th March 1819, depicts a dandy racing a John Bull figure along a country road. The idea also occurred to the Lewes correspondent of the *Sussex Weekly Advertiser*, who in his column for 31st May 1819 stated:

> At our ensuing races, we understand, that the Members' plate is to be restored; and we should like to see the Gold-cup subscription now in progress, extended sufficiently to afford a purse of twenty guineas for VELOCIPEDES, as it would introduce novelty – diversify the sport to the gratification of thousands – promote muscular exertion – give ample scope for betting amongst the black legs – bother the knowing ones – and furnish some dashing, athletic sprigs of fashion (after a due course of training for the purpose) with an opportunity of showing off, to the best advantage, before the ladies – and furthermore, it is *important*, that the character of the *Johnsonian Hobby* should be rescued from the disgrace and odium of DANDYISM.

The subsequent report of the Lewes Races contains no reference to any velocipede contest.

More positive steps were taken in Suffolk: "A subscription purse is to be run for on the first day of Ipswich races by *velocipedes*, five of which are already named and entered. The *riders* in jockey dresses, are to contend for the victory from what is called the Natton [this should be Nacton] corner of the racecourse to the winning post"[68]. The *Ipswich Journal*[69] tells us what happened:

> A great number of pedestrians and others ventured on the course, very many of whom got completely drenched by the heavy rain

---

[67] Published 24th March 1819.
[68] *Simpson's Salisbury Gazette*, 3rd June 1819.
[69] Saturday, 10th July 1819.

Fig. 46. *'Modern Pegasus or Dandy Hobbies in Full Speed'*, (1819 print, courtesy of Lewis Walpole Library). Both types of Johnson machine, direct and indirect steering, are depicted. The artist has omitted the arm rest or balancer which a Johnson machine would in fact have had.

which fell just as the horses started. The promised contest with Velocipedes, however, kept the company together after the race for the 100 gs. Three persons started for this prize, but so great was the eagerness of the multitude to be near them, that the riders, for want of scope, had no opportunity for showing their skill either in speed or jockeyism. Several persons with no other advantage than a nimble step, took the lead of them and kept it to the winning post.

It seems the new machine had become established at an early stage in this particular town, as we read[70] that: "The road from Ipswich to Whitton is travelled every evening by several pedestrian hobby-horses; no less than six are seen at a time, and the distance, which is three miles, is performed in 15 minutes". Speedy stuff if it can be believed!?

The situation at the Ipswich Races is very reminiscent of the occasion in Hyde Park three months previously (referred to earlier) when three velocipedists were "much impeded in their operations by the curiosity of the promenaders". Hopefully, the same problem was not encountered in connection with the much longer race on the outskirts of London[71]: "A grand velocipede match is spoken of between four amateurs. The distance to be 50 miles and to be decided on Blackheath. It is to be for a sweepstake of 25 guineas; the first to pocket the whole. The parties are in training".

There is an interesting paragraph in *Cowdray's Manchester Gazette* which reads:

> *Velocipedes.* We are credibly informed that Mr. W_____d, a Clerk in an eminent Solicitor's office in this town, is matched against Mr. C___ __n, in the same office, for 20gs. a side, to ride on a Velocipede twice round Kersall Moor; on Wednesday in the

---

[70] In *The Bury and Norwich Post* for 17th March 1819.
[71] Reported in Simpson's *Salisbury Gazette* for 6th May 1819.

race week, after the heat for the Gold Cup, by permission of the Stewards. We understand considerable sums are depending on the above match.[72]

The Manchester Meeting took place during the first week in June, but the newspaper does not report the result of the velocipede race. And a race involving "Velocipedes or Dandy Horses" was advertised in Sheffield for Monday afternoon 31st May[73], but it is not known whether the race actually took place. Nearer to the metropolis, we read[74] that "On Thursday next, at a Green near Bromley, a Velocipede Two-Mile Heat, for a handsome Cup, will be run, 2 to 1 against Rocket – Gimcrack against the field. Gentlemen may enter their Machines two hours previous to starting."

According to Helen Urquhart, curator of the Fife Folk Museum in Scotland, "Apparently there were hobby horse races in our village, Ceres". She cites a quote from a book[75]: "Close by the Habbie Horses flying around in their jing-go-ring". Helen Urquhart says the Andersons lived in one of the larger houses in Ceres, overlooking the green where the annual games are still held.

An "Extraordinary Race" which certainly did take place was between a rider of a hobby-horse and a rider on a donkey. The hobby-horse was in the lead for some while, but the jack ass was catching up when the machine and its rider "came down, when at full speed" with consequent damage to both, so that "the long-eared competitor" was declared victor[76].

The condition of the early Nineteenth century roads, coupled with the fact that (unlike the von Drais original) the English pedestrian hobby-horse had no brake, inevitably gave rise to accidents

---

[72] 1st May 1819.
[73] *Sheffield Mercury*, 29th May 1819.
[74] *Morning Chronicle*, 1st June 1819.
[75] *The Croft House Andersons* (1933)
[76] Reported in the *Nottingham Review* for 18th June 1819.

– particularly on downhill slopes. These are depicted in a number of the hobby-horse prints. As Thomas Davies put it in his 1837 lecture: "When the rider had acquired a certain velocity it became extremely difficult to turn the machine to the right or to the left, or even to touch the earth with either foot without instantly oversetting; and this difficulty of checking or stopping the machine at full speed ended in many accidents".

Davies says later that other evils arose: "If velocipedes ran on the foot pavements of the street, which they should not do, they got in the way of the children, or the children got in the way of them, and alarmed the ladies maids. Rash and heedless riders ran unluckily against fat people, and all fat men and old women cried out that velocipedes took up too much room on the pavement, especially if it was a narrow one."

The Sussex Weekly Advertiser contains reports of two velocipede incidents. On 26th April 1819 we read that: "A melancholy accident has occurred from the use of these newly invented machines. Monday, as two of these vehicles were descending the hill leading from Durdham Down to the Black Boy public house [in Bristol], with prodigious velocity, one of them came in contact with a lad at the bottom of the hill, who was thrown down by the force of the machine, which passed over his leg and fractured it in a dreadful manner. – The rider had not the humanity to take the least care of the unfortunate sufferer, but again mounting his velocipede (which had been upset), pursued his course with the greatest unconcern". In another report of the same incident we are told that "the father of the child has been making every effort to discover the author of his child's misfortune, but hitherto without effect".

The following week it was the turn of the hobby-horseman himself to suffer injury: "A gentleman at Farnham had the misfortune to have one of his arms broken by the fall of his Dandy Horse, which in going down hill got the better of him, and running in contact with a post, was thrown down with great violence".

Dashing Dandies

There is a further report of a serious accident in the Waterloo Road – presumably London. Two individuals had been racing together, one lost control of his machine, went over a bank and fell twelve feet, damaging the machine and dislocating his shoulder[77].

The Times newspaper[78] has an even sorrier tale to tell. "Mrs. Bearham, wife of Mr. Bearham, maltster, of Hunsley, Hants, returning home lately in her cart, the horse took fright at a velocipede, and she was thrown out and killed on the spot". The local newspaper gives the family name as Bareham and the place as Hursley (not Hunsley), which is near Winchester, adding "her loss is sincerely felt by her disconsolate husband and family, and a large circle of friends"[79]. This type of accident (hopefully not normally fatal) may not have been uncommon, and indeed throughout the Nineteenth century we read of the basic incompatibility on the road of the wooden or iron steed and its flesh and blood counterpart.

On a lighter note, we have a 'Whimsical Anecdote' under the heading 'A Mounted Tar capsizing a Host of Corruption'[80]. The print *Jack mounted on his Dandy Charger* (the frontispiece of the booklet) depicts the scene.

A more likely story is that recounted by the "very adroit pedestrian" referred to at the beginning of the previous chapter. He told how whilst riding his wooden horse he met a gentleman "on the highway by a river side, who, requesting to be allowed to try it, and being shown how he must turn the handle to guide it, set off with great spirit, but turning the handle the wrong way, soon found himself hurrying to the edge of the river; where, in his flurry, instead of trying the effect of turning the handle the other way, he began

---

[77] *Oxford University and City Herald*, 5th June 1819.
[78] 9th June 1819.
[79] *Salisbury and Winchester Journal*, 31st May 1819.
[80] On page 16 of Fairburn's *New Pedestrian Carriage* (see Appendix).

lustily shouting "woh! woh!" and so crying plunged headlong into the stream"[81]. The account is reminiscent of a reported incident in which "A velocipede ran away with its master a few evenings ago, and actually threw him into the dock, at Hull"[82].

In all probability accidents caused by hobby-horse riders gave rise to prosecution. Fairburn refers to one incident[83] where a dandy on his wooden horse charged a watchman, who retaliated by knocking him over, the dandy and his 'horse' being then detained overnight in the watch-house. But accident or no, hobby-horse riders were liable to prosecution if they rode on the pavement. Fairburn's little book[84] contains a most amusing item, the main details of which are corroborated in contemporary newspapers for March 1819. Captain Hoy has the last laugh in his legal battle with John Kendrick, the Beadle.

The Marlborough Street magistrate subsequently dealt with more cases. Under the heading 'Velocipedes'[85] we read: "A young gentleman, of fashionable fame [i.e. a dandy], was, on Monday, at Marlborough-street Office, charged with riding his hobby on the foot-pavement, and fined 40s. which he immediately paid". Another London prosecution for pavement riding again resulted in the standard £2 fine. The defendant said he was unable to pay as he had used all his money purchasing his 'charger' – which was accordingly confiscated with two days given to pay[86].

But the *Sussex Weekly Advertiser* records that: "Saturday, Wm. Harrison, Esq. was charged by several watchmen of the parish of

---

[81] *Howitt's Visits to Remarkable Places.*
[82] *Salisbury and Winchester Journal,* 7th June 1819.
[83] At the bottom of page 15.
[84] Pages 12 and 13.
[85] *Birmingham Commercial Herald,* 3rd April 1819.
[86] *Jackson's Oxford Journal,* 22nd May 1819.

St. Giles's with riding his hobby on the foot pavement from King street, Holborn, to Southampton row, Russell square. Mr. Harrison, in defence, said that the hobby horse was not on the foot pavement, but in the road. Several witnesses deposed to the same effect. The Magistrate (Mr. Farrant) ordered Mr. Harrison to be discharged, and the horse to be given back to him".[87] The case underlines the point that an offence was only committed under the Metropolis Paving Act if the machine was being ridden on the pavement, whatever over-zealous enforcers of the law might have wished to be the position.

The position seems to have been the same in some other parts of the country as well, perhaps under local Acts or bye-laws, as we read: "The magistrates of Bristol last week fined a person in the penalty of 20s. and costs, for riding a velocipede on the pavement of that city"[88]. The situation was the same in Cambridge[89].

The position in a neigbouring borough to Cheltenham (probably Gloucester or Tewksbury) deserves special mention. A notice published by an orthographically challenged Borough Surveyor reads: "This is to give notis to all persons that uses aney velosepeads or dandy chargers Either to Ride or wheel upon aney pavement or foot way within this burrow after this publick notis Information will be mad against them and the penalty imposed by an act of parliament will be levied upon them"[90]. The interesting point (apart from the Surveyor's spelling!) is to what Act of Parliament reference is being made, as this was sixteen years before section 72 of the Highways Act 1835 was passed, making it an offence to ride on a footpath by the side of a road.

---

[87] 26th April 1819.
[88] *Salisbury and Winchester Journal*, 21st June 1819.
[89] *Cambridge Chronicle*, 14th May 1819.
[90] *Cheltenham Chronicle*, 8th July 1819.

Fig. 47. 'The Female Race, or, Dandy Chargers running into Maidenhead' (1819 print, cliché Bibliothèque Nationale de France). The young ladies are clearly enjoying the ride - but why are they not wearing their riding breeches?

And it was not only the pavement from which the early velocipede was banned. At the end of May 1819 the Lord of the Manor of Berkhamsted, Herts, whilst agreeing that the game of cricket should continue to be allowed at the time of the Berkhamsted Sports, decreed that "women bruising for a prize, trap ball, quoits and Dandy Horses" were forbidden[91].

Hobby-horse riders were allowed on the King's highway, but what happened when they came to a toll-gate? There is a satirical depiction of the scene in the illustrated print *The Female Race! or Dandy Chargers Running into Maidenhead*. Later in the century there was to be considerable controversy as to whether cyclists should pay tolls, and if so of what amount. Perhaps it was a matter of serious dispute

---

[91] Quoted in *The Evolution of English Sport* by Neil Wigglesworth, London, 1996.

Dashing Dandies

Fig. 48. 'Military Hobbyhorse' (1819 print, author's collection). A military historian states the hobby-horse riders are wearing the uniform of the 12th Lancers, who are pursuing retreating French Dragoons.

when the two-wheeler first appeared on the road, but the author is only aware of the following anecdote[92]:

> A *Velocipeder* presented himself at a turnpike, and demanded, "What's to pay?" – That (said the waggish gate-keeper) depends upon whether you ride upon your hobby or pull it through; in the latter case, you know, a two-wheeled carriage drawn by any horse, mule or ass, is liable to the toll; and you will, I suspect, *come within the meaning of the Act.*

We know quite a lot about "the hobby-horse on the road", but what about the hobby-horse on the road to war? The received wisdom is that the bicycle was first seriously considered for military use in or about 1870, the earliest army cycling corps being established in England in 1888 and the first actual wartime deployment taking place during the Boer War 1899-1902.

But the idea of a military role for the newly-invented velocipede had surfaced in England as early as the spring of 1819. "The Velocipede is one of those machines which may probably alter the whole system of society; because it is applicable to the movement of armies, and will render rapidly practicable marches far more distant than have ever yet been undertaken"[93]. The illustrated print *Military Hobbyhorse* (Fig. 48) published by John Hudson dated 2nd March 1819, bears the legend "Particularly recommended to Cavalry Officers". And as we shall hear shortly, the idea of a corps of velocipedists was apparently at one stage under consideration.

In the event, the era of the pedestrian hobby-horse was a relatively brief one, and there was no significant military employment of the machine.

---

[92] Told in the *Sporting Magazine* for March 1819.
[93] *Monthly Magazine*, 1st May 1819.

Chapter 7

The demise and afterlife of the hobby-horse

Just then how brief was the hobby-horse era and what were the reasons for its decline?

Things seem to have been going well enough some four months after the machine was first introduced to the public at the beginning of the year. "Southampton, Saturday May 29. To such utility is the velocipede already advanced, that we frequently observe the arrival here of fanciful pedestrians from places 40 and 50 miles distant; their adoption is becoming very general in this town, and no inconsiderable degree of mechanical genius is evinced by the several juvenile persons who exhibit them"[94].

No doubt there were a variety of reasons why by about the middle of the year 1819 the invention began to fall into disuse. Some of the prints produced at the time caricatured the new machine, but others presented it in a favourable light, and in the author's view the role of the caricaturists in hastening the demise of the hobby-horse has been exaggerated.

The machine may have suffered from its association with the much despised dandies, even though dandies were by no means the only riders. It will be recalled that the *Sussex Weekly Advertiser*'s correspondent was concerned on this account ("it is important that the

---

[94] *Salisbury and Winchester Journal*, 31st May 1819.

character of the Johnsonian Hobby should be rescued from the disgrace and odium of DANDYISM").

The legal restrictions on the use of the vehicle were not particularly severe (though they must have acted as a discouragement to some extent), as they appear only to have prohibited pavement riding in London and in certain other towns and cities. The inherent mechanical restrictions of the machine, on the often rough roads at this date, must surely also have been a substantial reason for the decline in use.

A predominant reason why the machine fell out of favour may have been because it acquired a reputation for causing serious injury, and not only due to accidents. An amusing report appears in the *Birmingham Commercial Herald*:

> ROYAL COLLEGE OF SURGEONS, LINCOLN'S INN FIELDS. At a General Meeting of the Master, Governors, and Assistants of the Royal College, held at their Hall in Lincoln's Inn Fields, on Monday, May 10, 1819, a motion was made, seconded, and carried unanimously – That the Thanks of the College be voted to the inventors and multipliers of the VELOCIPEDES and ACCELERATORS, for the able assistance they are likely to give to the profession. Resolved also unanimously – That the said Vote of Thanks be written in the most beautiful manner on ASS SKIN, with the arms of the College emblazoned thereon[95].

In fact, the records of the Royal College of Surgeons show that there was no meeting of the governing body in May 1819, and the index covering the period 1811-1820 contains no reference to velocipedes. Nevertheless, a note in the *Sussex Weekly Advertiser* (and in other newspapers) reveals a genuine concern:

> IMPORTANT CAUTION. – The fatal efficacy of the Velocipede in producing ruptures has been formally announced by the

---

[95] 12th June 1819.

London Surgeons. An alarming number of cases of Hernia have within the last two months, offered themselves at the Hospitals of the Metropolis; all occurring among poor mechanics, who had indulged themselves in the Sunday use of this vehicle. In consequence of this most mischievous property, the amusement is much on the decline[96].

If the use of the hobby-horse velocipede was for health reasons "much on the decline" in August 1819, by the end of October of the same year it had "in consequence been laid aside", according to the *Monthly Magazine*[97]. The magazine refers to the fact that "the peculiar muscular action attending its frequent use causes ruptures and inflammations of certain muscles of the thighs and legs". The suggestion that on this account the use of the machine had entirely ceased would seem to be an over-pessimistic assessment of the position. It is nevertheless clear that the heyday of the pedestrian hobby-horse lasted for little more than six months during the year of its introduction.

By 1821 Lewis Gompertz of Kensington felt able to say that "it is worthy of observation how much delighted the public were with the velocipede on its first appearance, and how soon it was thrown aside as a useless toy"[98] – a description with which Gompertz himself does not agree. In his 1837 lecture 'On the Velocipede', Thomas Davies states "as is usually the case with every remarkable invention, it was not long before an outcry was raised against velocipedes. The old ladies remarked "They are such foolish looking things"."[99]

In his *Slang Dictionary* of 1823 'John Bee' (John Badcock), having defined the Dandy Horse as a "Velocipede or instrument for journeying far and fast: two wheels, one behind the other supporting

---

[96] *Sussex Weekly Advertiser*, 16th August 1819.
[97] *Mechanics Magazine*, 1st November 1819.
[98] In an article in *The Repertory of Arts*.
[99] Davies, T., *On the Velocipede*, 1837.

a bar of wood", says that "hundreds of such might be seen in a day: the rage ceased in about three years, and the word is becoming obsolete" (though in the same year John Atkin published his epic poem with its reference to a "dandy youth" who "rode on a velocipede"). However, Pinnock's *Catechism of Mechanics*, also published in 1823, discusses the principles of construction, action and management of the hobby-horse velocipede as a current not a historical phenomenon.

But having emphasized the relative briefness of the hobby-horse era, it is perhaps finally worth making the point that some machines continued in use, or were made and used, in a few corners of the realm right up to the late 1860s, when the pedaled 'boneshaker' came on the scene. During this period of nearly fifty years there were a variety of foot-treadled, hand-lever propelled and other velocipedes, mostly 'one-offs' or at any rate made only in small numbers, but these are really outside the scope of the present work. Our concern is with the hobby-horse (and its derivatives), in which the machine is propelled by pushing the feet on the ground.

There is an interesting passage in the 1869 book *Velocipedes, Bicycles and Tricycles* by 'Velox' (Tom Burgess):

> This brings us to the regular historic period of the introduction of velocipedes. Amongst those which were then introduced was [this one], sketched more than thirty years ago. It was rude and primitive in construction. A velocipede somewhat similar in construction was brought regularly into Northampton market from Yardley Hastings until a few years ago; but it was fancifully ornamented with gnarled pieces of wood in the form of serpents, snakes and animals; and one yet remains in the little village of Harpole, near Weedon, in the same county. The use of this machine caused a tendency to rupture, and, as accidents were frequent, it became neglected, and has long since been disused. It comes nearer to the 'Dandy-horse' – the well-known velocipede of fifty years since.

Fig. 49.   Non-steerable hobby-horse (from 'Velocipedes, Bicycles & Tricycles'). The milestone suggests the rider has ten miles to go to home.

The suggestion is that the machines referred to by 'Velox' may all have been of the non-steerable variety, though he avoids saying that they pre-dated von Drais and Denis Johnson. Indeed the specific machines to which 'Velox' refers appear to have been in use in the 1830s to 1860s period. The present author can vouch for the fact that a non-steerable hobby-horse does work (albeit as one would expect much less efficiently than the normal type), as he had the illustrated experimental model based on the illustrated 'Velox' sketch specially made for him some years ago. 'Steering' is achieved by forcing the rear wheel to skid to one side or the other, using one's body weight, or if a more major turn is required by simply lifting and moving the front wheel in the required direction.

The demise and afterlife of the hobby-horse

Fig. 50. Replica non-steerable hobby-horse, name of 'Oliver'. Made for the author. The wooden stand is of course removable.

Fig. 51. 'A meeting on the road from Layston Villa to Hormead Cottage' (watercolour by James Wilcox, 1849, Cyclists' Touring Club archive). The road configuration and windmill in the background, coupled with the artist's title, allow the exact location on the B 1038 one mile east of Buntingford to be established. The scene is little changed today, through the windmill has long since disappeared.

The demise and afterlife of the hobby-horse

Fig. 52. Mayfield family hobby-horse (courtesy of Hull Museum of Transport). Although it proved to be a trusty steed, this item lacks the stylish quality of the Johnson velocipede.

An exciting discovery was made by the author in the archive of the Cyclists' Touring Club. This is the watercolour depicting two velocipedists titled 'A meeting on the road from Layston Villa to Hormead Cottage'. The painting is signed by James Wilcox and dated 1st November 1849 (see Fig. 51). The four-wheeled machine appears to be hand-propelled, with the rider's feet off the ground, but the three-wheeler seems to be in the hobby-horse tradition with the rider propelling his velocipede as envisaged by von Drais and Johnson.

We also have some evidence with regard to the later use of the ordinary hobby-horse in connection with the illustrated example in the Hull Transport Museum (see Fig. 52). This is one of the few hub-steering machines known to the author, and like the example at Ipswich it would appear to be an approximate copy of a Johnson velocipede. A museum pamphlet dated 1905 records that the hobby-horse was donated by one J.W. Mayfield, who stated that his father, in his younger days, "frequently traversed the Yorkshire Wolds upon it", and that it was ridden "for many hundreds of miles", apparently last being used around 1860. The machine had originally been purchased at Scarborough by J.W. Mayfield's great-uncle, presumably in the hobby-horse era.

It is fascinating to read of a velocipede of this type owned by three generations of the same family (and ridden by two of them) throughout the greater part of the Nineteenth century. But this is not a unique situation. The recently discovered Johnson machine in the Pitt Rivers Museum (referred to at the beginning of Chapter 3) belonged to and was ridden by Lieutenant James Kirke, and later by his nephew Edward Mason Wrench, over a number of decades. It was finally donated to the Oxford University museum by surgeon Edward Wrench in 1905, when he refers to it in a letter as "the old family plaything".

A further interesting report of occasional use throughout much of the Nineteenth century is to be found in *Bicycles and Tricycles Past and Present* by Charles Spencer, apparently published in 1883. The author refers to "an ancient specimen of the Dandy horse, or original velocipede, at the establishment of Mr. Goy, 21 Leadenhall Street, London, to whose courtesy I am indebted for the following history of this very interesting machine".

Goy's was a long-established, well-known and successful 'Athletic Outfitter', who at this period was specialising in all cycling requirements. The item was apparently exhibited at the 1891 Stanley Cycle Show with other "ancient and historical machines which were lent for the occasion".

Spencer's account (courtesy of Goy) with regard to this "original velocipede" is:

> It was originally purchased by Mr. Frederick Roberts of Acre Lane, Brixton, at the sale of a deceased gentleman, Mr. Wilkinson, in the

year 1851. Mr. Wilkinson lived at Clapham Common many years ago, and he used to ride his Dandy horse round his grounds every morning. When Mr. Roberts bought it, in 1851, he soon found that when he appeared upon it in the public streets it attracted too much attention to be agreeable, and he was consequently compelled to restrict his practice to moonlight nights, when there were but few observers. Mr. Roberts says that the great objection to its general use was "the tendency it had for rupturing, and the labour of propelling it", but, he adds, "I used it, more or less, for years".

Additional evidence of the use of the hobby-horse substantially later than 1819 appears in the *London Bicycle Club Gazette*. The writer 'Goethe' tells us: "It was fifteen or sixteen years ago [1866 or 1867] that I first took to bicycling, and the machine was a real dandy horse, and many happy hours I squandered riding about on this glorious machine" [100].

At about the same time, John Burnett in his 1878 book *Useful Toil* quotes from an unpublished autobiography of Tom Mullins, a Staffordshire farm labourer who was born in about 1863. This includes the passage: "I saved my pocket money and bought a bicycle for 2s. 6d. It had a wooden frame and handlebars, but no chain or pedals, you simply pushed it along the ground with your feet". Tom Mullins would have been about seven to sixteen years old in the 1870s, and it was presumably during this period that he bought his hobby-horse for just 2s. 6d. – a tiny fraction of the £8-£10 paid for a Johnson machine more than fifty years earlier.

But after the pedalled 'boneshaker' was introduced into this country, half-a-century after the hobby-horse made its appearance, the earlier machine was no doubt usually regarded as little more than a curious relic. A report on the Barnes Common tricycle 'meet' in *The Cyclist* makes the point: "A gentleman, attired in the costume of a past age,

---

[100] 10th August 1882.

amused the spectators with riding a hobby-horse, built in 1819, about the Green"[101].

Although by the late Nineteenth century the hobby-horse was little more than a curious relic, Les Bowerman has drawn attention to an all-metal version of the machine, known as 'The Cyclopede', made by Mr. J.F. Bentley of Ludgate Circus (London) and sold for just £3. At an even later date, in the late 1920s and 1930s, a Mr. Windbridge of Banwell, an employee of Cooper, Mobley & Co. of Birmingham, was apparently making hobby-horses for sale in his spare time. Presumably he saw a market for such inexpensive machines at this time of economic depression.

An interesting, recent hybrid development is the 'Kickbike' scooter, made in Finland. It looks like a conventional bicycle at the front, but has a small rear wheel with no saddle or drive mechanism and is propelled from a standing position like a scooter. And an example of a modern child's hobby horse (there are others) is the LIKEaBIKE, produced in Germany and available in various models. It is good to see the original velocipede in use again, as a way to teach a young child to ride on two wheels, as an alternative to the child's tricycle, or bicycle with stabilisers.

---

[101] 10th August 1882.

Chapter 8

The Dandies and other riders

The price of Denis Johnson's patent pedestrian machine was normally between eight and ten pounds, a large amount in 1819 for a beam on two wheels. In his advert notifying the appointment of a Leeds agent, Johnson states the price for his machines is "from 8 to 12 Guineas, to be paid on Delivery". The higher figure perhaps indicates that where necessary the item was slightly more expensive to cover agent's commission and transport costs. Only the reasonably well off could afford such an extravagance, though many more took to the road on hired machines. But the Dandies and the Nobility – including Royalty – were it seems its principal purchasers.

According to *The Slang Dictionary*[102] the dandy was "a fop, or fashionable nondescript … DANDIES wore stays, studied a feminine style, and tried to undo their manhood by all manner of affectations which were not actually immoral". *The Oxford English Dictionary*[103] says the term was in vogue in London from about 1813 to describe the 'exquisite' or 'swell' of the period.

Certainly the expression was well-established before the pedestrian hobby-horse arrived on the scene. A disconcerted lady wrote to the *Sporting Magazine* in March 1817 telling of the visit of a smart young gentleman down from London. A party of youngsters was arranged to entertain him, when during a game of "innocent romps" he was observed to have a pair of stays on. The lady wrote: "On

---

[102] 1874 edition.
[103] 1989 edition.

this circumstance being mentioned to one of my acquaintance, she said he was only – a *Dandy*. – Now Sir, I am quite ignorant what a Dandy is, or of what sex a Dandy may be, and should be glad if any of your correspondents could inform me: because – because (I am sure, I am quite ashamed when I think of it) if I was to marry something in a pair of stays – though they may call it a Dandy, it would be no consolation to me. – As I cannot subscribe my real name, I must sign myself, EMILY DOUBTFUL. Hempstead, Essex."

Lest there should be any doubt as to the extent to which a Dandy might go in his attempts to out-do the 'fair sex' at their own game, we are told in the *Sporting Magazine* that: "The lodgings of a *dandy* were lately robbed of a pair of *stays*, a *smelling bottle*, two pairs of artificial *eye-brows*, and a white surtout, in a pocket of which there were *three love letters*, written to himself, in his own handwriting!"[104] During the following six months the magazine contains an amusing 'Diary of a Fashionable Dandy', an article 'Misfortunes of a Dandy', a poem 'The Dandy' and an article on 'A modern Narcissus'.

Simpson's Salisbury Gazette has an item 'On the Fluctuations of Fashionable Phraseology' which is even more disparaging: "The modern *Dandy* has usurped the place of the *Beau*, the *Buck* of former years. Its external character – a pair of stays – high heeled boots – short waist – starched cravat – narrow brim'd hat – sans sense, sans brains, sans wit, sans everything that a man should possess. Its specific character – vast self-importance – selfishness the ruling principle – affecting to despise all things not within the pale of the Dandy community, exactly as they are unaffectedly despised by all wise and respectable persons" [105].

These, then, were the individuals who eagerly took to the hobby-horse on its arrival on the London scene in the spring of 1819. There

---

[104] August 1818.
[105] 15th April 1819.

The Dandies and other riders

Fig. 53. Enamelled hobby-horse pill box (author's collection). An appropriate accoutrement for the Regency dandy. However, it would not have been possible for him to have owned this particular one, as it was it seems made by the Parisian maker Samson, founded in 1845. The item possibly dates from the 1890s or a little later.

Fig. 54. A fob seal for the dandy's chain – two views. The message 'EVERY ONE HAS HIS' and the 'hobby' image are of course in reverse in order to produce the correct impression on the wax. (Courtesy of Lorne Shields.)

103

can be little doubt as to the extent of their patronage, as the very name 'dandy-horse' sometimes used to describe the new machine shows. A lengthy letter with the title 'The Dandy and his Hobby' in the *Hull Packet* is quite specific on the point: "It was for their [the Dandies] accommodation that that wonderful animal, the Long-Acre charger, was first brought out of its native woods"[106].

In the light of the supposed effeminacy of these Regency beaux, it seems surprising that they were prepared in such numbers to undertake such energetic exercise as the velocipede required, and to take the risk of falling off and even of serious accident or injury. Perhaps we should revise our opinion of these young gentlemen, on the basis that you can't always judge the contents of a parcel by its packing. *The Birmingham Commercial Herald* contains the following amusing account (though Mr. Lund may not have found it funny at the time):

> THE UNFORTUNATE DANDY. On Friday afternoon, about one o'clock, four gentlemen, mounted on their hobbies, undertook for a wager of one guinea to run a race from the Half-way-house, Lower-road, Deptford, to Chinahall, being a distance of half a mile. On coming facing Mr. L.'s, the Cottage of Content, which is about mid-way, and where there is an angle in the road, Mr. Lund, who was second, attempted by an act of dexterity to drive before his leader, when, going too near the bank, which sloped downwards, he was precipitated head foremost into the ditch, and was completely covered over with the mire, which stuck to him like pitch. He was taken into Mr. L.'s, where he was washed and cleaned, and accommodated with a change of clothes, until he sent home for others. His companions seeing the accident, did not proceed on their journey, but deferred it to another opportunity[107].

The important illustrated print *Johnson's Pedestrian Hobbyhorse Riding School* (Fig. 33), appears to provide a portrait of one particular dandy.

---

[106] 8th June 1819.
[107] 5th June 1819.

According to Dorothy George: "In the foreground on the extreme right a dandy walks forward; he resembles Lord Petersham"[108]. Lorne Shields has noticed that this individual is remarkably similar to the dandy in the illustrated print *The Dandy Charger* (see Fig. 77). If this surmise is correct, we can conclude that Lord Petersham was a hobby-horse rider. In any event, as late as 1874 it is still recalled that "Lord Petersham headed them" i.e. the dandies[109].

It is probably Lord Petersham who is the hero (or perhaps anti-hero) of *Hobbyhorsiana*, a light-hearted contemporary account of the dandy and his 'charger' by 'Joe Dobbin', who is referred to as "a biped blood horse of the true breed, and a member of the new rocking-horse university". His Lordship is described in the opening paragraph of the booklet as follows:

> IN a small parlour, furnished in the first style of fashion, sat Lord P_____ over his breakfast. His red hair, to the oiling curling and brushing of which he had devoted the best part of an hour, was surmounted with a green silk nightcap; his elegant form was obscured by a roomy surtout, his feet were enclosed in Turkish slippers, with toes turning up somewhat after the Chinese fashion, and his body filled out a large arm chair with some dignity.

A dandy was nothing if he was not showing off, and Johnson's machine allowed him to do this in some style. The author of *Hobbyhorsiana* explains "How to make yourself conspicuous":

> Paint your charger all manner of queer colours, and spot your face with blacking. Instead of a hat, wear a red night-cap, to which, instead of a tassel, hang a few rush-lights; turn your coat inside out, and wear the seat of your breeches in front: then wheel along the street with a hymn book in your hand, and sing as loud and merrily as though you had a whole nest of nightingales in your

---

[108] In the British Museum *Catalogue of Political and Personal Satires*.
[109] *The Slang Dictionary*.

Fig. 55. 'The Dandies' Rout' 1820 (reproduced from 'A Nursery Companion' by Iona & Peter Opie, courtesy of Oxford University Press). The artist's simplistic representation of the machines seems appropriate for a nursery rhyme.

belly. This has such an imposing effect, that all those who are influenced by outward appearances, mark you down as a very spirited fellow, whose acquaintance deserves cultivation; and as for those lovely young creatures called females, let them be ever so pretty, their tender affections can never withstand the wink of so important a personage.

The dandy and his hobby-horse even featured in a nursery rhyme of the period, written by eleven-year-old Caroline Sheridan, granddaughter of Richard Brinsley Sheridan[110]. The verse accompanying the above drawing reads:

> A hobby-horse apiece, they all
> With speedy steps go to the ball.
> Their wives and daughters there they'll meet,
> The Dandizettes so mild and sweet,

---

[110] The illustration by Robert Cruikshank of three individuals on their machines is from *The Dandies' Rout* (the word is used in the archaic sense of a social gathering), originally published by John Marshall in 1820.

> As you will soon have an example,
> In my Lady Fimple Fample.

Amongst the relatively better off it was not only the dandies who were affected by the hobby-horse fever. According to a late source: "Fox, Sheridan, Pitt and other notabilities of the period, patronized the velocipede in St. James' Park, taking the constitution daily on the Dandy Horse, after a hard night spent in the House of Commons or around the gaming tables"[111]. However, little weight can be given to this statement as Charles James Fox, statesman and orator, had died in 1806, the same year as the Tory prime minister William Pitt the Younger, and the dramatist and politician Sheridan (Caroline's grandfather) had died ten years later, some three years before the hobby-horse came into use. Perhaps it was their ghosts seen riding in the park on their spectral machines!

A 'notability of the period' who in his late-forties *did* apparently ride the hobby-horse was the famous poet Samuel Taylor Coleridge, of 'Ancient Mariner' and 'Kubla Khan' fame. Entry 4543 in *The Notebooks of Samuel Taylor Coleridge* commences: "Mile End, Bow, Stratford, Ilford, Chadwell, (Heath opposite), Rumford, 12. Road velocipedous throughout – dry, hard, level and dustless. Sat. June 8, 1819"[112] and goes on to detail other rides, with the times taken to accomplish them. The speeds of between eight and nine miles an hour claimed by Coleridge are fast – but by no means impossible on a 'velocipedous' road.

We know of one young hobby-horseman who went on to become a famous politician in later life, the Right Honourable Robert Lowe M.P., Chancellor of the Exchequer from 1868 to 1873 (and later Viscount Sherbrooke). *The Dictionary of National Biography* (now the *Oxford DNB*) records him as being an "ardent advocate of

---

[111] *The English Mechanic* for 1868.
[112] Routledge, 1990.

Fig. 56. The Right Hon. Robert Lowe M.P. In his youth a master of the dandy-charger, in later years Chancellor of the Exchequer in the first Gladstone administration.

bicycling". As President of the West Kent Bicycle Club he made a speech on 15th September 1887[113] in which he stated, after referring to the introduction of the velocipede: "I had the honour in the reign of [George IV] of riding one of these machines, so that I may term myself an ante-bicyclist or anticipator of the bicycle. I was considered quite an adept at the exercise, and remember once riding a mile race on one of these dandy-horses with His Majesty's mail, and contriving to get in before it to my infinite delight". As Robert Lowe was born at the end of 1811, he would only have been seven years old in the spring of 1819, and even at the end of the reign of George IV he was still only eighteen.

---

[113] Reported in *Bicycling News*.

The Dandies and other riders

Fig. 57. 'The Parson's Hobby – or Comfort for a Welch Curate' (1819 print, author's collection). According to Dorothy George, the extreme poverty of the Welsh clergy was a traditional theme.

109

Fig. 58. Silhouette of the Rev. Joseph Coltman on a velocipede (author's collection). A popular image reproduced as a postcard formerly available at Beverley Minster, also as a print.

Puzzlingly, the nephew of Lieutenant James Kirke (referred to in a previous chapter) says that his uncle frequently raced with Robert Lowe, each mounted on his hobby-horse, on the Great North Road between Newark and Tuxford. As this cannot have been much later than 1820, *if correct*, the future Chancellor must have been one of the youngest serious riders of the velocipede.

As referred to previously, "Clergymen used the new machine to visit their parishioners, and to travel between scattered parishes". There is indeed a satirical 1819 engraving published by Tegg, *The Parsons Hobby – or Comfort for a Welch Curate* (see Fig. 57), on precisely this topic. The Reverend Joseph Coltman, M.A., J.P., 1776-1837, Vicar of Beverley Minster, Yorkshire, for almost a quarter of a century, was a real life example. The earliest date the illustrated silhouette of this oversize gentleman astride his machine could have been produced is spring 1819, when Coltman was already forty-two years old. Unlike the majority of riders, it would seem that he employed his velocipede regularly for many years, perhaps until his death at age sixty, as a note written thereafter states this was his "favourite mode of travelling".

The Reverend Coltman was a highly gifted individual, much loved by his parishioners – an elaborate memorial inscription extolling his virtues can be seen in Beverley Minster. It is said that at one time he weighed as much as 43 stone, although 37½ stone is the figure usually quoted. Apparently Joseph Coltman actually rode his machine into church, as it seems that it became the only way he could transport his enormous bulk (when not travelling in his carriage). As walking up the steps to the altar was impossible, a board was placed sloping from the floor of the nave up to the pulpit. Coltman rode to a convenient spot where three vergers were waiting to receive him. The head verger 'took aim', and the three together rushed the priest up into the pulpit.

There are also accounts of Coltman travelling round his parish on his hobby-horse assisted by a boy who pulled on a rope attached to the machine (which on other occasions travelled with him in his carriage), and of his "trusty old servant" helping him to mount and dismount and "keeping his inanimate charger in the highest possible condition". It is reported that one occasion Joseph Coltman fell into a ditch whilst riding his velocipede.

Further details of Coltman's life (and an early portrait) can be found in various publications in the Beverley Reference Library. There is also a brief biography in *John Markham's Colourful Characters*[114].

An eccentric but affable Cornish curate the Reverend William Spry lived in Penzance but officiated at the parish church of St Levan (1815-1826). He acquired a hobby-horse, and according to one source[115] used it "when deemed necessary" to transport himself to his cure some nine miles away. Another source provides colourful

---

[114] Highgate Publications (Beverley) Ltd., 1992.
[115] 'The Parish Church of St Levan' www.stlevanchurch.co.uk.

Dashing Dandies

Fig. 59. Dandy-horse playing card (author's collection). Grandfather on his early two-wheeler. One of six 'Cycling' items from a card game probably dating from the mid-1890s.

details of racing and two early accidents suffered by the parson on his 'horse', with the consequence that he "never trusted his wooden horse to make such long journeys any more".[116]

The extent to which children were able to ride the new machine has been a matter of conjecture. However, some light has been thrown on the topic by letters written in the spring of 1819 by the Rev. John Hodgson to his wife in Northumberland, whilst he was visiting London. He informed her he went with friends "to see the dandies riding on hobby-horses; or, as they are called, velocipedes". He was not impressed, commenting that the contraptions were

---

[116] *Traditions and Hearthside Stories of West Cornwall, vol.1,* by William Bottrell (1870), reproduced at www.sacred-texts.com.

"mere whirligigs and playthings, fit only for boys to ride on under 10 years of age".

A further letter makes it clear this was not just a meaningless, disparaging comment. The reverend gentleman tells his wife: "The little boys about London are all getting dandy-horses, for such seems at present the name of the Velocipede: I wish Richard and John could see one of them; as for Richard, he would never know how to guide it, but John, I think, in a year or two's time, will be able to master it, though it will move only on level ground."[117] Rev. Hodgson's younger son John was just five years old at the time, so the suggestion was that when he was six or seven he would be able to ride the machine.

---

[117] Letters dated 28th April and 18th May 1819 in *A Memoir of the Rev. John Hodgson* by James Raine, vol. 1, 1857, pp. 216 & 247.

Chapter 9
Stage antics and Royal patronage

At the beginning of the hobby-horse craze the machine received considerable attention at the London theatres. Indeed, according to 'Square Toes': "It made its first appearance on the English stage, in conjunction with an appropriate character, in the late Covent Garden Pantomime, and has since become generally known to the town, by our artisans who fabricate vehicles, and our artists who furnish the designs, which attract the gazers at the principal shop windows".[118]

The Covent Garden Pantomime *Harlequin Munchausen, or, The Fountain of Love* ran from Boxing Day 1818 to mid-February 1819 (with a final performance on 1st March), which certainly suggests a very early public display of the item, even if it was not introduced into the script at the very beginning of the run. The probability is that the "appropriate character", who presumably rode a hobby-horse on stage, was the enormously versatile and popular English clown and pantomimist Joseph Grimaldi, who played 'My lord Humpy-Dandy' in the scene entitled 'The Chateau of Sir Hilario Frosticos'. The illustrated print *My LORD Humpy Dandy!!* depicts the character as performed by Grimaldi (see Fig. 60).

The new machine was also to be seen at an early date at the Theatre Royal, Drury Lane. A playbill dated 8th February 1819 for the pantomime *The Silver Arrow: or, Harlequin and the Fairy Pari Banon*

---

[118] Letter in *The Kaleidoscope* for 23rd March 1819.

Fig. 60. 'My LORD Humpy Dandy' (1819 print, courtesy of Lewis Walpole Library). "As performed by Mr. Grimaldi in the pantomime of Harlequin Munchausen at the Theatre Royal Covent Garden". Below the print are the words of a song describing the 'Dandy Beau'.

reads: "in the course of the Pantomime will be introduced a NEW SCENE, wherein the Harlequin, the Pantaloon, and Clown will RIDE A MATCH on Horses capable of travelling at the Rate of Ten Miles an hour, which never eat or drink, never tire, and are so gentle and tractable that a Child seven years old may manage them, and when tired of riding may carry them under his arm".

In April, the Epilogue of *Comedy of Honour* at the Drury Lane Theatre concluded with about twenty lines on the new machine, referring to the author's hopes in appropriate terms: "Hobbies, he hears, are now the mode accounted, So for nine nights, at least, he hopes he's mounted"[119]. The following month the Epilogue to *Carib*

---

[119] There may also be a reference to Lord Petersham – "Should one of you – perhaps his dandy lordship – be riding past".

Chiefs by The Hon. W.R. Spencer was almost entirely given over to the hobby-horse, and concluded:

> Our Cocknies now shall fear no break-neck tumble
> On steeds that never start, and seldom stumble;
> And hunters only one small danger find,
> To break their horses *wheels*, and not their *wind*.
> Then for our *letters* - Oh the sweet invention!
> And Johnson well deserves a *Palmer's* pension!
> Bus'ness or Love may travel by express,
> With speed far greater, and expense far less,
> On wood scarce thicker than a witch's broomstick.
> Laden with news I see the Hobby *groom-stick*
> Speed the soft intercourse from soul to soul
> And weft a sigh o'er England – on a pole!
> Our *"wooden walls"* were long the Patriot boast –
> Soon *wooden cavalry* shall be our toast;
> And when some WELLINGTON to conquest leads
> Our new-built squadrons of – Velocipedes,
> What foe will dare our prowess to withstand,
> Borne on our native oak o'er sea and land![120]

The suggestion that Johnson "deserves a Palmer's pension" perhaps requires explanation. In 1784 John Palmer began operating a mail-coach service, which was subsequently expanded and greatly expedited the delivery of the post. For this public service he was eventually granted a state pension and other benefits. The suggestion now made is that the Johnson velocipede could be employed to even greater effect, and so entitle our hero to a similar reward. A suggestion which appears to have been adopted – perhaps on a trial basis and with only limited benefit to Johnson – the following year.

In June 1819 the patrons of the Covent Garden Theatre's production of Sheridan's *School for Scandal* were regaled with a speech by

---

[120] *Simpson's Salisbury Gazette*, 27th May 1819.

"Mr. Liston, riding on a Velocipede", playing the part of a dandy and favourably comparing the hobby-horse to the "living steed", concluding with the stirring words:

> Methinks I see Newmarket's glories fade –
> Egham and Ascot sink into the shade.
> No more the mettled Courser's swift career
> Shall fire the soul of Commoner or Peer:
> Brittania's Horsemen, for a bit of wood,
> Have barter'd their old boast – *their bits of blood.*[121]

And as late as the beginning of July, a comic song 'An attempt at an impossibility', referring to "London Fashions, Follies, Dandies, and Hobby Horses" was performed by Mr. Knight at the Theatre Royal, Drury Lane[122]. And an advertisement refers to the publication of 'The Dandy Charger: or, Cock-Horse A-la-Mode. A satire. By B. Read':

> Turn out troops Farmer Dobson – calls his wife –
> I ne'er se'ed such a horse in all my life!
> Look! my belief its head's dropt off! and 'fegs,
> It runs main well with ne'er a tail nor legs[123].

The only other known contemporary song on the topic has the title 'The Perambulator or Pedestrian Hobby Horse' (see Fig. 61). It has four verses praising the new machine. The expressed hope that "the inventor will soon disclose, A hobby for Ladies too", suggests a publication date of around April 1819, as Johnson's lady's version became available the following month.

The only known engraving with a thespian theme is the illustrated *New Reading – or – Shakspeare Improved* (published by Thomas Tegg). One of Edmund Kean's principal roles was as Richard III in

---

[121] *Sporting Magazine*, June 1819.
[122] *Liverpool Mercury*, 2nd July 1819.
[123] *Morning Chronicle*, 12th July 1819.

Fig. 61.   'The Perambulator or Pedestrian Hobby Horse' (song cover). The composer J. Alford sung the song "at the public entertainments".

Shakespeare's play of the same name. The king is made to proclaim the words "A Hobby! A Hobby! my Kingdom for A Hobby!!!". The print is "Humbly Dedicated to the Keen Critic of Drury Lane, by a poor Author" (see Fig. 62). This would appear to be a reference to the very public and acrimonious dispute between Keen and the playwright Bucke, whose tragedy *The Italians* the celebrated actor described as "the worst of the bad".

A number of the hobby-horse velocipedes still in existence belonged to the aristocracy. Machines were owned by Sir John Leicester of Tabley House, the Duke of Marlborough of Blenheim Palace, the Duke of Northumberland of Alnwick Castle, the Earl of Durham of Lambton Castle, the Earl of Eglinton of Eglinton Castle in Scotland, the Duke of Argyll of Roseneath Castle, also in Scotland, and the Duke of Leinster of Carton House in Ireland. In the last century machines have been owned by Sir Philip Brocklehurst and Sir Edward Iliffe, which may have been in their families for several generations.

But whilst the pedestrian hobby-horse clearly achieved a measure of popularity amongst the titled class, one must be careful in drawing a conclusion from the fact that they owned a not insubstantial proportion of the extant machines. This can to some extent be explained on the basis that such artefacts were more likely to survive within the confines of a stately home, remaining in the ownership of the same family for many generations. It is nevertheless clear, on the basis of the evidence of the successors to Denis Johnson's firm that "the *accelerator* was much used by the nobility in the early part of the present century and brought many patrons to their predecessors"[124].

Two Johnson hobby-horses (numbered 299 and 300) are still to be seen at the Duke of Northumberland's country seat at Alnwick

---

[124] Letter in *Bicycling News*, 17 September 1880.

Dashing Dandies

Fig. 62. 'New Reading – or – Shakspeare Improved' (1819 print, author's collection). Unlike the 'Military Hobbyhorse' print, only wooden horses are to be seen on the field of battle.

120

Castle. They were ancient relics nearly 170 years ago, when Howitt wrote volume 2 of his *Visits to Remarkable Places in 1841*. He was told the story of how the 'pranks' of the Duke's 'horse' caused it to be "disused and stabled". "The Duke and his physician used to amuse themselves with careering on these steeds about the grounds; but one day, being somewhere on the terrace, His Grace's Trojan steed capsized, and rolled over and over with him down the green bank, much to the amusement of a troop of urchins who were mounted on a wall by the road to witness this novel kind of racing".

The Duke of Northumberland's machines may well have inspired what is by far the longest versification on the subject of the hobby-horse. The poem, printed at Alnwick in 1819, is again simply called 'The Velocipede'. It tells in no less than fifty six-line verses how Tom Stirabout, "a dandy of prime merit" (whose friend was a Marquis), had been forced to sell his horses to pay his debts and decided to acquire a more affordable wooden horse instead. He goes to a shop to inspect the machines, tries one and immediately falls off, much to the amusement of the shopkeeper and his staff. The shopkeeper offers tuition in a field nearby, where "the painted charger was upon the ground". The poem concludes:

> Led by the shop boy, firmly on his seat
> Tom sat; and us'd, as precept taught, his feet.
> Till, bolder grown, triumphantly he utter'd,
> "Give him his head; I see that I can do it";
> Though as he spoke, his very heart-springs flutter'd, -
> There was a hill, and he had just come to it.
> The instant it departed from the level
> Down ran the dandy-charger like the devil.
>
> Tom loudly roar'd, (whilst down ran lad and master)
> Cursing Velocipedes with all his soul:
> The pertinacious frame work went the faster;
> But near the bottom pitch'd into a hole;
> Its headlong speed could then no further go,
> And Tom performed a *volti subito*.

His head was proof; and Heaven most kindly granted
That part should *first* arrive upon the green;
So (as some castigating lash was wanted)
A broken leg was all that clos'd the scene:
And Tom was homeward carried from the hill,
With scarce one doit to pay the doctors bill[125].

Fairburn's *New Pedestrian Carriage* contains[126] an amusing description of a race through London between two members of the aristocracy, under the heading 'A Race from Alpha-Cottage to Tyburn'. As with the 'Mounted Tar capsizing a Host of Corruption' referred to earlier, it is not easy to decide whether the event being recounted is fact or fiction or a mixture of both, though further research might well provide the answer.

It is again from Fairburn that we learn of the Prince Regent (later George IV) as a patron of the hobby-horse. His principal interest was in flesh-and-blood fillies – and not only the equine variety as we shall soon learn. But whilst the present author has so far been unable to come across any reference to the Prince Regent actually riding a machine, either in London or Brighton (where he spent much of his time at his Pavilion remodelled by John Nash), there seems no reason to doubt Fairburn's account of four machines being sent down from (presumably) London to the Prince's seaside home. Corroboration of a wider royal interest is to be found in *The Freeman's Journal* (Dublin) where it is stated that the Accelerator (a commonly used term for the hobby-horse in Ireland) was "patronized by several of the Royal Family" [127].

As one might expect, the Prince Regent's seaside base became the terminus for journeys on the new machine. *The Times*[128] records that

---

[125] Printed at Alnwick in 1819 and sold for 'Price Twopence'. The poem is called simply 'The Velocipede'.
[126] Page 15.
[127] *Freeman's Journal*, 12th April 1819.
[128] 9th June 1819.

"Mr. T. Alford (presumably a relative of the J. Alford who composed the hobby-horse song) and three others, travelled lately on a velocipede from London to Brighton (50 miles) in 9 hours". And we learn that: "It is now become quite common for persons to come down to Brighton from London on *Velocipedes*"[129].

But whilst it seems clear that for a time the Prince Regent (now in his mid-fifties) took a keen interest in the new machine, there is at present no reason to suppose that this in fact progressed beyond the acquisition of the four examples referred to by Fairburn. Some years ago, the author was in touch with the Director of the Royal Pavilion at Brighton, who had no knowledge of the present whereabouts of any of the machines.

It appears that the Prince Regent's younger brother, the Duke of York, also owned a hobby-horse. Fairburn tells us "As £10,000 per annum is not sufficient to maintain a *prince's horse*, one of *Johnson's Chargers* has been bespoke to convey the royal duke *once a month* to Windsor". This requires a little explanation. In January 1819 the Duke of York was nominated by his brother to the sinecure of *Custos Personae Regis* (guardian of the King's body), which apparently involved little more than a regular trip to Windsor to visit his ailing father George III. For this the Duke received an indeed princely sum of £10,000 per annum. Perhaps not surprisingly the appointment met with much disapproval, and a number of satirical prints portray this as a miserly attempt to save travelling expenses. The illustrated print *Economy – or a Duke of Ten Thousand* is a good example (see Fig. 63).

The British Museum catalogue of prints contains references to more than a dozen satirising the Prince Regent and the Duke of York, depicting them as velocipede riders. A number show the Prince with his supposed mistress Lady Hertford. The illustrated engraving

---

[129] *Simpson's Salisbury Gazette*, 10th June 1819.

Fig. 63. 'Economy – or – a Duke of Ten Thousand' (1819 print, author's collection). The Duke of York on the road to Windsor to visit his ailing father George III. A gold bag – no doubt a bag of gold – contains his annual salary for the task.

Fig. 64. Staffordshire pottery jug (courtesy of Sotheby's Sussex). The machine depicted is again likely to be an invention of the caricaturist, though we know that von Drais had the idea of a tandem machine. A plate of similar design is discussed in an article 'Fine and Dandy' by Alison Petch of the Pitt Rivers Museum, Oxford (available online, with an 'alternative view' by the present author).

A P****e, Driving his Hobby, in Herdford!!! is typical (see Fig. 65). According to Charles Carlton in his book *Royal Mistresses*: "Wrinkles did not discourage the Prince, for, as one court gossip noted, older dames seemed to be his taste"[130]. In 1819 Lady Hertford was in her sixtieth year (the Prince was a couple of years younger). The

---

[130] Routledge, 1990.

Fig. 65. 'A P****e, Driving his Hobby, in HERDFORD!!!' (1819 print, courtesy of British Museum). The Prince Regent and his Lady friend both appear to be enjoying the ride. But this hobby-horse is of course a fiction of the caricaturist's imagination.

Stage antics and Royal patronage

Fig. 66. Willem, Prince of Orange's velocipede - two views (courtesy of the House of Orange-Nassau Historic Collections Trust and of the National Cycle Museum of The Netherlands). Clearly based on the Johnson machine, the most noticeable differences being the armrest support and handlebar stem. The backbone close-up shows the mark of Queen Anna Paulowna (wife of Willem II, previously the Prince of Orange), who died after her husband and presumably inherited the machine.

127

print strongly suggests a sexual connection, but in fact although their relationship was a long-standing one, according to Dormer Creston in *The Regent and his Daughter*: "It is thought that she never actually became his mistress, but, whether she did or not, she risked the appearance of being so"[131].

Publication of the affairs of the royal brothers went beyond these prints. Another of the Prince's favoured ladies was the Duchess of Richmond. The illustrated Staffordshire pottery jug[132] depicts the Duke (presumably) and Duchess of Richmond on a long-backed hobby on 'A Visit from Richmond to Carlton House', the Prince's London residence (see Fig. 64). The Duke of Richmond died from the bite of a rabid fox in the latter part of 1819.

But it was not only English royalty who took to the English version of the Draisienne. The House of Orange-Nassau Historic Collections Trust at The Hague has a hobby-horse which belonged to the Dutch royal family – this being indicated by the frame mark 'A' below a crown. According to Gertjan Moed, Director of the National Cycle Museum of the Netherlands, the presumably original owner of the machine was the Prince of Orange (later King Willem II), who used to ride it in the park of his hunting seat Soestdijk in Baarn. The Prince was born in 1792, so would still have been a young man at the date the hobby-horse was probably acquired around 1820. Although as can be seen from the illustration (Fig. 66) it is very similar to a direct-steering Johnson machine, the maker's name stamped in three places is T. Kerr. Nothing is known about this individual.

---

[131] Eyre & Spottiswoode, 1932.
[132] Sold at auction by Sotheby's, Sussex, in June 1991.

Chapter 10
Two and three-wheelers for the fair sex

Whilst there is little direct evidence that ladies actually rode hobby-horses, the circumstantial evidence is overwhelming. The contemporary booklet *Hobbyhorsiana* contains several references to the riding of hobby-horses by ladies. Firstly, there is an illustration of a 'Ladie's Dandy Hobby' straddled by a skirted female rider – the road sign points to 'The New Way to Strechit'. The machine is virtually identical to the normal 'Gentlemen's Dandy Hobby' also illustrated in the booklet. Then, in a report of a supposed lecture on the velocipede which starts by categorizing the new machines, we read of: "A Lady's Horse. This is a truly elegant machine, the back is in general formed of wood, and either plated, gilt, or painted with variegated and elegant devices. The saddle is made soft by a horse-hair stuffing and a covering of red velvet, whilst the saddle cloths are, for the most part, either made of silk or satin and richly embroidered".

Finally, at the end of the booklet we have: "Rules for the Fair Sex. If my fair countrywomen should feel ambitious of emulating the male sex, she must remember that the Velocipede will not admit of her sitting sideways. No, no, females are at length put to such an extremity that they must wear the breeches whether they be shrews or not; therefore, on with a pair of yellow leathers and top-boots – on with them, I say, and mount your chargers strideways, like the gentlemen. Then roll away like a billiard bowl, throwing

Dashing Dandies

Fig. 67. 'FASHIONABLE EXERCISE, or The Ladies Hobby School' published by J. Johnstone in 1819 (courtesy of the Bibliothèque Nationale de France). Clearly the long skirts of Regency times were a problem when riding the machine designed for gentlemen.

130

your legs elegantly to the right and left, captivating the heart of every gentleman who passes you, by the grace of your motions and attitudes".

One of Denis Johnson's two pedestrian hobby-horse riding schools may have been given over in part to teaching the 'fair sex' the art of velocipede management. The illustrated print *FASHIONABLE EXERCISE or The Ladies Hobby School* (see Fig. 67) is both satirical and salacious, unlike the straightforward engraving *Johnson's Pedestrian Hobbyhorse Riding School* illustrated earlier. But as we have seen previously the satire may sometimes have a basis in reality, and the author suspects this may well be the case here.

We know that Johnson had riding schools both at 377 Strand and at 40 Brewer Street. The illustrated print *Views of the Lady's Pedestrian Hobbyhorse* states the machine depicted "is now exhibiting at 40 Brewer Street" (the gentleman's version was on show at 377 Strand) (see Fig. 68). It seems reasonable to surmise that the Brewer Street premises were also used as a ladies riding school. If this is so, the engraving is likely to date from around April 1819, as we know that the gentlemen's school probably started in March and the ladies' one is unlikely to pre-date it. The gentleman's machine illustrated would presumably have been replaced in the ladies' school by the one specially designed for them when this became available.

An advertisement for Johnson's exhibition in Bristol (referred to in Chapter 4) is addressed specifically to 'The Ladies of Bristol' and states: "Mr. JOHNSON particularly invites the Ladies, because he fears, from their known delicacy, they may debar themselves from that gratification which the perfections of the Vehicle are highly capable of imparting". Clearly there had been a reluctance on the part of the female sex to ride the new machine. An item in the *Bath & Cheltenham Gazette* tells us: "The Patentee *is adapting* [author's italics] the power of this machine to the use and pleasure of female

Fig. 68 'Views of the Lady's Pedestrian Hobbyhorse' (12th May 1819 print, author's collection). The only known surviving print of the ladies' version of the Johnson machine.

riders",[133] but the ladies' version may not have actually become available until the following month.

The new velocipede was not the subject of a separate patent, but this expensive exercise may have been considered unnecessary in view of the protection supposedly afforded by patent no. 4321 of 1818. The machine's main feature was a dropped frame to allow for the long skirts worn by the ladies of the period[134]. John Fairburn tells of the new machine's imminent arrival on the scene in his booklet. At the very end Fairburn states: "There is now constructing a Charger for females of the same nature – wood and paint – for the use of the ladies, it is to be named the ANTI-STRADDLING CHARGER."

The legend below the Ackermann lithograph (see Fig. 68) of 12th May 1819 *Views of the Lady's Pedestrian Hobbyhorse* explains the item as follows:

> THIS MACHINE is an ingenious apology for the Ladies: it possesses equal power with the Gentlemen's, will turn as short, and is not so liable to upset, having the perch below instead of above. It is of the most simple kind; two light wheels running on the same line, the front wheel turning on a pivot, which, by means of a short lever, A, fig.1 gives the direction in turning to one side or the other; the hind wheel always running in one direction. The Rider being conveniently seated on the small square board B, leans forward against a well-padded cushion C, which terminates with a cross balance-board D, on which the arms rest, to balance the Machine if inclining too much either way: in this position the drapery flows loosely and elegantly to the ground, whereupon the feet are placed as in walking, so that in the first step to give the Machine motion, the heel should be the part of the foot to touch the ground, and so on with the other foot alternately, as if walking

---

[133] Bath & Cheltenham Gazette, 21st April 1819.
[134] A modification re-introduced at the end of the Nineteenth century when women took to riding safety bicycles.

Fig. 69. Lady's hobby-horse (Science Museum, Wroughton). The general aspect shows that the item as made was very similar to the contemporary print (see Fig. 68).

on the heel, observing always to begin the movement very gently (see Fig. 68).

How many of these machines were made is not known. The only surviving one of which the author is aware is the illustrated Science Museum exhibit, which is in its store at Wroughton, Wilts. The item appears to be in substantially original condition. It has 30" wheels and is said to weigh a relatively heavy 66lbs. Both the seat and the body and arm rest are adjustable, an improvement on the gentlemen's machine (where only the height of the saddle can be altered). Conservation work carried out at the Science Museum has revealed that the original colour was dark brown with white coach lining.

There were several other machines designed specially for the use of ladies in 1819. None seems to date from earlier than May, three months or more after the gentleman's version first became known. All these machines were three-wheelers, and as such would not presumably have infringed the Johnson patent. The best known today is

Two and three-wheelers for the fair sex

Fig. 70. Lady's hobby-horse (Science Museum, Wroughton). The finial and curly steering rod are typical Johnson, though the 'St. Paul's dome' has become a beehive.

Fig. 71. Lady's hobby-horse (Science Museum, Wroughton). The arm and body rest are fully adjustable.

135

Dashing Dandies

Fig. 72. 'The Ladies Hobby' (1819 print, author's collection). If the print is to be believed, half-a-dozen such machines could be seen together at one time. The author suspects this may be wishful thinking – but maybe not while the item was 'all the rage'. The number of prints depicting the machine lends some support to this view, as does the fact that plates, jugs and mugs illustrating it were also produced.

probably the Pilentum[135], otherwise known as the Lady's Accelerator or Ladies Hobby. The illustrated print *The Ladies Hobby*[136] (see Fig. 72) is one of several depicting the machine. The method of propulsion is explained at the base of another print with virtually the same title in the following terms:

> The principle of this Machine consists in two boards acting on cranks, on the axle of the fore-wheel, in a similar manner to those used for the purpose of turnery, and is accelerated by the use of the handles, as represented in the plate; the direction is managed by the centre handle, which may be fixed so as to perform any given circle.

Although this three-wheeled velocipede was mechanically inefficient to the modern eye, at the time it must have appeared to be a real advance on the hobby-horse driven forward by placing the rider's feet on the ground. Indeed it came tantalizingly close to the much later pedalled machine of the 1860s – in essence only requiring foot pedals to be added to the "cranks on the axle of the fore-wheel" in substitution for the complicated arrangement depicted. Another print refers to the machine as having been invented by Hancock & Co. of St. James's Street and exhibited at 97 Pall Mall. The caption reads: "This elegant little vehicle is peculiarly adapted for the use of the Ladies, as well as Gentlemen. It is impelled, by the slightest touch of either the hands or feet, at a rate truly astonishing; and is so completely secured from upsetting, that the most timid person might use it with the greatest confidence"[137].

A further machine produced by Hancock & Co. was the 'Enneapheron'. This unusual item "calculated for parties of pleasure or performing journeys" was made to carry nine persons (an

---

[135] The word is from a carriage of this name apparently used by the Roman ladies and referred to in the *Aeneid*.

[136] Dated 22nd May 1819, published by Tegg.

[137] *A Pilentum* published by S. & J. Fuller.

Fig. 73. 'Pilentum' plates (author's collection). The smaller one is less than 5½" diameter and carries the message "Of Dandyzets the queen In her accelerating machine" and the description "The newly invented PILENTUM".

enneagon is a polygon having nine sides). It was exhibited with the Pilentum at 97 Pall Mall[138].

Another three-wheeler is described in *The Gentleman's Magazine* for June 1819 in the following terms: "Lady's Velocipede. A model of a velocipede, invented for the use of ladies, is now exhibiting at Ackermann's, in London. It resembles Johnstone's [sic] machine, but has two wheels behind, which are wrought by two levers, like weavers' treadles, on which the person impelling the machine presses alternately with a walking motion. These move the axle by means of leather straps round the cramps; and the wheels being fixed revolve with it. The lady sits on a seat before, and directs the velocipede as in the original invention". Unfortunately, there appears to be no extant print or drawing of this item, but the notion of propelling a tricycle by means of rods or levers turning a cranked axle between two rear wheels was employed on a number of occasions during the early and middle years of the Nineteenth century.

We have seen earlier that the Royal supposed mistresses were dealt with by the hobby-horse artists in a less than sympathetic manner. There are a number of other prints depicting attractive young ladies riding (or preparing to ride) ordinary hobby-horses which were obviously produced to titillate the male libido. One blatant example is *FASHIONABLE EXERCISE or The Ladies Hobby School* referred to at the beginning of the chapter. The groom peeping round the curtain at the two half-dressed young women, whilst holding the hobby-horse in a suggestive manner, says: "Now Ladies! if either of you is ready I have got hold of the primest thing in the school. Its christened the Favourite".

The illustrated print *The Female Race! or Dandy Chargers running into Maidenhead* (Fig. 47.) is not much better. The figureheads of dandies on the front of the machines ridden by the ladies make it clear that we are looking at a variation of the *equus eroticus* theme.

---

[138] Advert in *The Morning Chronicle* for 12th July 1819.

The foremost rider says: "We have 'em in Maiden head at last! Who would have thought that we should be able to drive them so far into the Count ry on the first trial?". There are several more engravings of a broadly similar (if not quite so scurrilous) nature, involving sailors, undergraduates – and even Quakers!

There is one print which in the author's opinion does provide further corroborative evidence of actual hobby-horse riding by ladies. This is the illustrated George Cruikshank engraving *The* Hobby *Horse Dealer*. The lady rider in the background is incidental to the main subject of the illustration and is drawn in a perfectly straightforward manner. It seems reasonable to assume that the artist was depicting a known and perhaps not too uncommon situation. The lady appears to be riding the distaff version of the Johnson machine (see Fig. 74).

Some three-wheel velocipedes were designed to have women as passengers and not riders. Possibly the most successful was the "Velocimanipede, or Lady's Hobby", invented by a London coachmaker Charles Lucas Birch and marketed by him in May 1819. This is shown in the print *More Hobbies, or the VelociManipede* (see Fig. 75). The machine was described in *The Times*[139] in the following terms:

> It is calculated to accommodate three persons: the front compartment is constructed in the same manner as the common velocipede; the centre consists of a convenient seat, fitted up like the seat of a jig; and the third portion is behind the centre, in the shape of a dicky. It is worked by the person in front and the person behind, the person in the middle sitting perfectly easy. The man in front has work of the same kind to do as the rider of the common velocipede, the one behind sits in the dicky, with his feet supported by a foot board, and the exertions he has to make is to turn the wheels beside him: for this purpose a handle is fixed to the axis of

---

[139] 13th May 1819.

Two and three-wheelers for the fair sex

Fig. 74. 'The Hobby Horse Dealer' (1819 print, courtesy of Lewis Walpole Library). The Johnson hobby-horse is critically examined as if flesh and blood. A respectable lady leads the background riders.

141

Dashing Dandies

Fig. 75. 'More Hobbies, or the Veloci Manipede' (1819 print, author's collection). One of four known prints illustrating Birch's invention, which was exhibited before royalty. An amusing contemporary comment was that: "The Velocimanipede is not likely to take with either male or female dandies, as being anagrammatised, it says, I can impede love".

each wheel, and which is turned round in the same manner as a common hand-mill. The machine combines ingenuity with use, and must produce admiration. It is particularly available in private roads and gentlemen's parks.

The Velocimanipede (i.e. a velocipede to be worked by hands and feet) was exhibited by Birch to the Duke and Duchess of Kent in the grounds of Kensington Palace on the afternoon of 11th May 1819: their Royal Highnesses were duly impressed. The following month the inventor was to be found displaying his machine in the grounds of Marlborough House when the Duchess of York was visiting Prince Leopold. Clearly Charles Lucas Birch knew the right people. The newspaper report on this later occasion[140] confirms that "the centre, or chaise-seat" was "intended for a lady". The vehicle was claimed to do eight miles an hour with ease.

Another three-wheeler with a seat for a fair companion is shown in the illustrated April 1819 print *The New Invented Sociable, or The Lover and his Hobby* (see Fig. 76). It is a matter of speculation whether this machine was ever in fact seen in England. The engraving is an Anglicised version of an 1818 French print entitled *Vélocipède Sentimental!! ou Draisienne Francaise*. Karl von Drais had the original concept.

It is impossible to estimate the extent of actual female participation in the hobby-horse craze, either as riders or passengers. The fact that a number of machines were produced exclusively or primarily for ladies, does not of course itself indicate that they achieved any degree of popularity. It would however be somewhat surprising to find at least three makers, including the astute businessman Denis Johnson, all attempting to sell velocipedes for which there was absolutely no market. It seems reasonable to conclude that there must have been some use of the new machines by the fair sex, but that for the most part the riding of velocipedes was regarded as a male prerogative.

---

[140] *Sussex Weekly Advertiser*, 28th June 1819.

Dashing Dandies

Fig. 76. 'The New Invented Sociable, or The Lover and his Hobby' (1819 print, author's collection). Von Drais recommended such machines to be used on wide, level promenades in good condition. The family man at the foot of the hill stands no chance. And the chances of survival of the apparently wooden-legged hobby-horse rider on the way down must be regarded as slim!

144

Chapter 11
The hobby-horse prints

The story of the pedestrian hobby-horse is brought vividly to life by about eighty prints published in London (and a few also in Dublin), largely during the first half of the year 1819. The author knows of no English depictions of the machine before February 1819, and only three after September of the same year (published around November 1819, November 1820 and August 1821).

Oddly enough, one of the best collections is to be found in the Département des Estampes of the Bibliothèque nationale de France in Paris, where there are more than sixty English prints, ignoring duplicates (in addition to a number of Continental ones). These are part of the substantial collection of "engravings, drawings, water colours, etchings or other pictures" depicting various types of early transport, bequeathed by the pioneer motoring enthusiast Sir David Salomons of Tunbridge Wells to the French library "in memory of the kindness and courtesy I always received in that country".

The Coventry Transport Museum has about fifty items, and the British Museum has a similar number of prints in the Department of Prints and Drawings. The Canada Science and Technology Museum has some forty prints, as does the Lewis Walpole Library of Yale University. The Library of Congress, Washington DC, has about thirty prints. Examples may also be seen in the John Johnson collection at the Bodleian Library, Oxford, and at the Science Museum, South Kensington. The author himself has some thirty-five original items.

Most of these prints measure about 8" (20cm) x 12" (30cm), but there is no absolutely standard size and a few items, for example those from magazines, are considerably smaller. The great majority are hand-coloured engravings, but there are a few lithographs and aquatints. Impressions of the same print can be found with completely different colourings. Illustrations of all the known prints, with notes on each one, will be contained in the author's planned book *Before the Bicycle*.

It has often been said that a major reason for the demise of the hobby-horse was the scorn poured on it in the many prints published and sold in London in the spring of 1819. This is an over-simplification of the position. The illustrations can be divided into three broad types. Firstly, those in which the velocipede is depicted simply as a phenomenon of current interest, without any hint of ridicule or satire. Secondly, those in which the prime intention is indeed to pour scorn on the new machine and the dandies and others who rode it. Thirdly, those in which the satire is really political (including attacks on royalty), the hobby-horse being merely a convenient and topical means by which the message could be portrayed.

Some of the most attractive prints fall within the first category. The well-known Rudolph Ackermann – whose premises in the Strand were opposite Johnson's riding school – was the publisher of a number of items depicting the pedestrian hobby-horse in a sympathetic manner. The *Pedestrian Hobbyhorse, Johnson's Pedestrian Hobbyhorse Riding School*[141], *Johnson, the First Rider on the Pedestrian*

---

[141] Drawn by Henry Alken, a noted exhibitor at the Royal Academy. There were two original versions of the *Johnson's Pedestrian Hobbyhorse Riding School* print, both dated 10th March 1819 and stated to be published by Ackermann, with no artist named. The only difference is that one had a six-line description of the machine and how to ride it at the bottom of the print. It is in fact the same wording as is below the well-known *Pedestrian Hobbyhorse* print, published by Ackermann on 1st February 1819 in his *Repository of Arts*. It appears from Ackermann & Johnson records that Ackermann sold the copper plate of the version without   *continued*

Hobbyhorse, and *Views of the Lady's Pedestrian Hobbyhorse*, have all been referred to previously and are illustrated. The author's own version of the *Riding School* print is uncoloured, but there are also a number of differently coloured imprints known. It is interesting to speculate whether Ackermann was simply taking an independent and sympathetic interest in the hobby-horse velocipede, or whether there was a direct financial link between him and Denis Johnson, with the object of providing favourable publicity. The author suspects the latter, and this view appears to be shared by the French cycle historian Jacques Seray.

John Hudson of 85 Cheapside was the publisher of half-a-dozen well-drawn prints, all but one of which appear to be by the same artist, William Heath, identified only by his monogram 'WH' in one of the drawings[142]. Hudson was active throughout the early part of 1819 when most of the engravings and other items were being produced, his *Modern Olympics*[143] (on the cover of this book) being the earliest in the British Museum collection, with the illustrated print *The Dandy Charger* bearing the same date. *The Ladies Hobbye* is dated 21st May 1819, *More Hobbies, or the Veloci Manipede* dates from 18th June 1819, and the unillustrated *An Unexpected Occurrence* has the relatively late date of 17th August 1819 (and is probably not by Heath).

There is an interesting link between the well-known Ackermann print *Pedestrian Hobbyhorse* and Hudson's *The Dandy Charger*, both dating from February 1819 (see Figs. 43 and 77). The Bibliothèque Nationale has a copy of an untitled, unascribed and undated print based on the Ackermann one, apparently by William Heath. We have

> this description to another publisher in 1819. A third version bearing a publication date of 17th April 1819 names Henry Alken as the artist, but does not name the publisher. What seems to be the original copper plate of this third version was acquired in 2003 by Lorne Shields from a London dealer.

[142] *Military Hobbyhorse*, 2nd March 1819.
[143] Print dated 23rd February 1819.

Fig. 77. 'The Dandy Charger' (1819 print, courtesy of Lewis Walpole Library). The association of the pedestrian hobby-horse with the dandies came at a very early stage. This print is dated 23rd February 1819.

the same woodland scene, but this time the rider is depicted coming down a slope at some speed. The dandy figure astride the machine is identical to the one in *The Dandy Charger*, but in reverse. Presumably this untitled print also dates from about February 1819.

Another attractive first category print is *Match against Time or Wood beats Blood and Bone* (see Fig. 78). The legend below the drawing provides a potted history of the pedestrian hobby-horse in a single sentence: "This famous *Hobby* was bred in Germany after winning every thing there was Shipd for Long Acre Patronized by the Dandies and is now Expected to out run all the First Blood on the Turf"[144].

---

[144] Published 17th April 1819 by Thomas Tegg of 111 Cheapside (artist's name not shown).

Fig. 78. 'Match against Time or Wood beats Blood and Bone' (1819 print, author's collection). Both riders are similarly attired as horse jockeys. The actual velocipede riders at the 1819 Ipswich Races were to be "in jockey dresses".

Thomas Tegg was probably the most prolific publisher of hobby-horse prints (twenty are known), most falling into the second category i.e. taking a humorous view of the machine and its riders, varying from scenes of mild amusement (the illustrated *Going to the Races*), to those of outright opposition or ridicule (the illustrated *Anti-Dandy Infantry Triumphant or the Velocipede Cavalry Unhobby'd*). About half the prints in the author's own collection are published by Tegg.

The letter from 'EVAC'[145] (referred to in Chapter 8) refers to the opposition to the hobby-horse by vested interests: "It is said that the hostlers at the different inns have come to a resolution of not attending on the outlandish German animal, for as it lives on less than a straw a-day, it entirely deprives them of their perquisites. It will, I think, be dangerous to ride these animals in the country, for the farmers cannot sell their oats since the introduction of these foreign hobbies".

The opportunities for wit provided by the advent of the hobby-horse were many and various. Several prints show a variety of imaginary machines based on the hobby-horse idea. The illustrated *Every One His Hobby Plate 1* and *Plate 2* are good examples (see Figs. 82 & 83). The parson rides his bible, the lawyer his brief, the doctor his pestle and mortar, the sailor his anchor, and so on. A cheery John Bull sits astride his 'rump of beef' with a tankard of 'porter' in his hand.

This latter image was copied onto a two-handled pottery jug (Fig. 81). This is rather a puzzle piece since the item bears the date *1872* and is inscribed *J. Wilson. Police Sergeant. W.R.C. Normanton*. The puzzle lies in the correct dating of the item. In view of the motif it might be thought that it dates from 1819 and not the later date, the jug having been over-painted in 1872, in order perhaps to be presented to Sgt. Wilson of the West Riding Constabulary. However, the probability is that this is a retrospective item using an 1819

---

[145] *Hull Packet*, 8th June 1819.

The hobby-horse prints

Fig. 79. 'Going to the Races' (1819 print, author's collection). Note that again the team of five hobby-horsemen are all dressed in jockey uniform.

Fig. 80. 'Anti-Dandy Infantry Triumphant' (1819 print, author's collection). According to a contemporary New York newspaper: "Horses, it is said, in England, have fallen in price 10 per cent, in consequence of the sudden appearance of these velocipedes". The author would require more evidence to support this assertion.

The hobby-horse prints

Fig. 81. Two-handled pottery jug, circa 1819 (author's collection). The author will be pleased to hear from anyone who is able to supply further information on Sgt. J. Wilson of the West Riding Constabulary.

image, and that it does indeed date from 1872. This view is shared by china expert Noël Riley.

As we have noticed previously, a number of the hobby-horse prints can reasonably be seen as having erotic undertones. The illustrated print *The Master of the Ordnance exercising his Hobby!* is a good example (see Fig. 84). An even more blatant example is the illustrated 1819 print *Boarding School Hobbies! or Female Amusement!* There are no hobby-horses to be seen, but the reference in the title and the date of publication clearly justify the inclusion here (see Fig. 85).

153

Dashing Dandies

Fig. 82. 'Every One His Hobby, Plate 1' (1819 print, author's collection).

154

Fig. 83. 'Every One His Hobby, Plate 2' (1819 print, author's collection). Only the dandy is riding a regular machine.

Fig. 84. 'The Master of the Ordnance exercising his Hobby!' (1819 print, courtesy of the Canada Science & Technology Museum). Wellington is featured in Plate 1 of 'Every One his Hobby', but this depiction is less innocent. A young lady onlooker remarks "Bless us! what a Spanker! – I hope he won't fire it at me – I would never support such a thing."

The hobby-horse prints

Fig. 85. 'Boarding School Hobbies! or Female Amusement!' (1819 print, courtesy of British Museum). A variation of the 'equus eroticus' theme, or (as Dorothy George puts it) "Governesses and pupils bestride giant cocks".

157

Fig. 86. A man and woman on hobby-horses. Courtesy of Lorne Shields of Canada. This unique watercolour shows an ordinary couple on a countryside road. The item is undated.

There were in fact a variety of plates, jugs, snuffboxes and other items with velocipede motifs produced during the hobby-horse era. There are a number of illustrations of hobby-horse plates in Noël Riley's 1991 book *Gifts for Good Children: the history of children's china 1790-1890*. There is even a fragment of tapestry depicting a Johnson hobby-horse at a museum in France. All these items are now very collectable. What may well be the only surviving extant contemporary watercolour of a woman and man riding hobby-horses is illustrated (Fig. 86).

A very large hobby-horse jug was sold at a Bonhams auction in May 2006. It commemorates the union of the Prince Regent's daughter Princess Charlotte and Prince Leopold, but the main illustrations are of the Pedestrian Hobby-Horse, the Lady's Accelerator and five caricatures from the print *Every One his Hobby Plate 2*. The jug has the caption 'Richard Cooper's Hobby Red Lion St Helen' (Richard

Fig. 87. Large commemorative hobby-horse jug. Courtesy of Lorne Shields. Princess Charlotte, the only child of the Prince Regent and his wife Caroline of Brunswick, died following childbirth in November 1817. She was mourned by the whole nation. The jug carrier is the author's wife Trish.

Cooper was the landlord of the Red Lion, St Helens, in 1819/1820 and probably earlier) has a circumference of 3'2" (almost a metre), carries 47 illustrations (most are repeated) – and holds 25 pints of foaming ale! (Fig. 87).

But to return to the prints. Tegg was certainly not the only publisher to pour scorn on the velocipede. The print *Enough to make a* Horse *Laugh! or The World upon Wheels* (Fig. 88) is by J. Sidebethem, who like Ackermann was based in the Strand. Seventeen Sidebethem prints are known, which makes him the next most prolific publisher after

Dashing Dandies

Fig. 88. 'Enough to make a Horse Laugh! or The World upon Wheels!!' (1819 print, author's collection). More horse than hobby-horse in the picture, but the satirist's point is well made.

160

Tegg. But whereas Ackermann's early print *Pedestrian Hobbyhorse* shows the principal rider smartly dressed propelling his machine purposefully through an Arcadian countryside, Sidebethem is far less respectful. Both the horse in the foreground and his liveried groom view the hillside scene with great amusement. A dandy is kicked off his mount by a braying donkey. A lady and gentleman have apparently been involved in a collision and lie on the ground on top of their machine, the gentleman losing his hat and wig. A rider careers downhill seemingly out of control of his hobby. And in the background we see more riders speeding downhill (one falling off), whilst others are climbing back up with their machines on their shoulders.

Sidebethem's *Enough to make a* Horse *Laugh!* print has the name '(Yedis)' beside that of the publisher, which according to Dorothy George may indicate that Sidebethem himself was responsible for this illustration, possibly with Robert Cruikshank as the engraver. George suggests that 'Yedis' may be a pseudonym for Sidebethem, employing the first four letters of his name reversed, preceded by the letter 'Y' (perhaps 'Bedis' would have been too obvious). An interesting tale is told by Charles Spencer[146] with regard to Sidebethem's relationship with Cruikshank (no Christian name is given but the reference to "not then a teetotaller" suggests Robert's more famous brother George, who became teetotal). It purports to explain why both James Sidebethem and Cruikshank became distinctly unsympathetic to the new walking machine. The story goes as follows:

> Cruikshank was on very friendly and intimate terms with his publisher, James Sidebethem, and on one occasion, in the winter of 1819, the two cronies, dressed in the extreme of the preposterous fashion of the day, set forth on an excursion, each on his hobby-horse. All went well for a considerable distance, but when coming down Highgate Hill at full speed – at a rate of nearly ten miles an

---

[146] In his circa 1883 book *Bicycles and Tricycles Past and Present*.

hour – the riders "cannoned", or "collided", to use the expressive Americanism, and away they went, each falling with considerable violence on an opposite side of the road, the result being that the machines sustained serious injuries, while they themselves were severely shaken. Mr. Cruikshank (who it is to be presumed was not then a teetotaller) was led by his friend, who was the less injured of the two, into the Archway Tavern, where they obtained as much consolation as was possible under the circumstances, finally returning to London on one of Wiber's coaches.

Spencer concludes that Cruikshank's subsequent "droll sketches of mournful-looking individuals" were "exhibited in Mr. Sidebethem's window in the Strand, and promptly excited the risibility of passers-by to such an extent that it became positively unsafe to appear in public on a Hobby-horse, so loud and universal was the laughter at the resemblance in the street and his caricature in the shop window". The present author suspects this may be something of an exaggeration of the true position, though there is plenty of evidence to suggest that, particularly when the machine made its first appearance, it engendered much idle curiosity. The illustrated print *The Pedestrian Carriage, or Walking Accelerator*, with its descriptive narrative, published by Sidebethem, is in no way derogatory, but would presumably be early and perhaps pre-dating the Highgate Hill episode (see Fig. 89).

Another second category print is the illustrated *Dandies on their Hobbies!* (see Fig. 90). This is of particular interest as the Tate Gallery has the preliminary sketch from which the print emerged (see Fig. 91). The publisher of the print was Sidebethem, and as 'Yedis' as previously stated he may also have been the artist. Coincidentally, the author himself has recently obtained what remains of the preliminary sketch for a print with the short title *A New Irish Jaunting Car* by Robert Cruikshank (see Figs. 92 & 93). As can be seen from a comparison of the illustrated items, the print (the reverse of the drawing) omits the central fat man figure in the sketch.

The hobby-horse prints

Fig. 89. 'The Pedestrian Carriage, or Walking Accelerator' (1819 print, courtesy of the Canada Science & Technology Museum). This engraving forms the basis of the illustration of the machine on the Denis Johnson commemorative plaque at 75 Long Acre.

163

Dashing Dandies

Fig. 90. 'Dandies on their Hobbies!' (1819 print, courtesy of British Museum). The foreground machines all have two rear wheels close together (see earlier comment on the 'Pedestrians travelling' print). The seat for the lady is an invention of the artist to add erotic interest.

164

The hobby-horse prints

Fig. 91. Preliminary sketch for 'Dandies on their Hobbies' (1819, courtesy of Tate Gallery). It is interesting to compare this with the final printed version, where the image is of course reversed.

165

Dashing Dandies

Fig. 92. 'A new Irish Jaunting Car' (1819 print, author's collection). Dorothy George says that the lime kiln in the background suggests the fields around London.

166

Fig. 93. Preliminary sketch for 'A new Irish Jaunting Car' (1819, author's collection, a gift from Peter Card). It is a pity that the drawing has been cut down, but the main part still remains.

The most numerous prints in the third category – political satire – are those relating to the Prince Regent and his brother the Duke of York, which have been referred to earlier. Apart from these, there are relatively few concerning political issues of the day. One example is the illustrated *The Chancellors Hobby, or More Taxes for John Bull*[147]. The engraving depicts Vansittart, Chancellor of the Exchequer, astride a large green bag representing the budget, running down the archetypal citizen John Bull. The reference is apparently to the additional taxes to reduce the national debt proposed in Vansittart's Budget (Fig. 94).

Another illustrated attractive third category print is *The Devil alias Simon Pure*, subtitled *Say's the King of the Radicals "Hurt not the soldiers"*. This item is of particular interest as it is dated August

---

[147] Published by Tegg and dated 19th June 1819.

Dashing Dandies

Fig. 94. 'The Chancellors Hobby, or More Taxes for John Bull' (1819 print, author's collection). One of relatively few expressly political prints. The signposts point "To ruin", "To Starvation" – and "To America".

168

1821, and is accordingly the latest known hobby-horse velocipede engraving. The Johnsonian hobby-horse is equipped with a stand (which can also be seen on two of the surviving examples) (see Fig. 95).

According to Dorothy George: "On 11th September, the subject of the print, one Charles Wheatfield Squires, presented a paper containing this caricature to the Lord Mayor, saying that a copy had been sent to Lord Bathurst (Secretary for War). He was dressed as a Quaker, with a beaver hat and tricolour cockade, as in the print. For some days he had been conspicuous in London, having come to town on a velocipede with a plan which "it was given out, will astonish and benefit the nation when it is divulged"."[148] Dorothy George adds that: "Accounts of his eccentricities appeared in the papers and he was identified by his brother as insane". Whether the riding of a pedestrian hobby-horse was by 1821 regarded as a sign of insanity is not stated! Simon Pure was a Quaker character in Susannah Centlivre's 1718 play *A bold stroke for a wife*.

Squires (referred to simply as 'a Quaker') put in an unscheduled appearance at Bow Street magistrates court on 27th September 1821. He insisted that a large packet was delivered to the magistrate Mr. Minshull. It was found to contain "a sort of political caricature, in which the Quaker himself was represented riding on a velocipede over the necks of certain well-known persons", entitled 'The Radical Quaker', and other works of a similar nature. He had a strange conversation with the magistrate and then left[149].

There were quite a number of different publishers issuing hobby-horse prints in London in the year 1819. It is useful to understand the relationship between the artist, the engraver (or lithographer), the printer and the publisher. In many (but by no means all) cases, these four roles were filled by just two individuals. According to John

---

[148] Item 14234 of the British Museum *Catalogue of Political and Personal Satires*.
[149] *The Morning Chronicle*, 29th September 1821.

Dashing Dandies

Fig. 95. 'The Devil alias Simon Pure' (1821 print, kind permission of Coventry Transport Museum). The reference immediately under the title is to Queen Caroline, the estranged wife of George IV. She was forcibly prevented from attending his coronation in July 1821 and died the following month.

170

Wardroper in his introduction to *Cruikshank 200*: "The prints were etched on copperplate, generally by the artist himself, and printed on a small press behind the shop"[150]. In some instances (J.L. Marks of Bishopsgate is an example), the print shop owner not only printed and as publisher sold the items, he was on some occasions also the artist and engraver.

In addition to the many London publishers (apparently for the most part print shop owners), McCleary of Dublin produced quite a number of prints, other Dublin publishers being T. Lepetit and Clayton. These items seem to have been copies – pirated or otherwise – of items first published in London. There was indeed something of a hobby-horse craze in Ireland in the spring of 1819, with at least two firms making machines and opening riding schools in Dublin[151]. *The Dublin Journal*[152] commented: "Pedestrian Accelerator. Some of these Ingenious Machines are now to be seen in Dublin, and plates of them appear in all the print-shop windows".

Until recently, there were known to be two original machines remaining in the Republic of Ireland. The illustrated item (Fig. 96) with attractive ornamental iron supports to the balance board belonged it is said to the Duke of Leinster of Carton House, County Kildare. It was apparently acquired from the Estate of the then Duke of Leinster in 1942, having it seems for many years been stored in a dry loft over the coach house in the stable yard. The other (unillustrated) machine would appear originally to have been owned by John Talbot Power of the Dublin distilling house of John Power and Son, which started business in 1791. The design of the front and

---

[150] The 1992 catalogue of the travelling exhibition to celebrate the bicentenary of George Cruikshank's birth.
[151] The full story is told in the author's paper 'King Chrononhotonthologos and All That' (subtitled 'The Hobby-Horse in Ireland'), published in volume 15 of the Proceedings of the 15th International Cycling History Conference, held in Vienna in September 2004.
[152] 12th April 1819.

Fig. 96. Duke of Leinster's hobby-horse (courtesy of 'Velorama'). The sprung saddle is adjustable for both height and position.

rear forks and saddle spring suggests that this is a less ornate version of the Duke of Leinster's velocipede.

Most of the hobby-horse prints were unsigned and unattributed, making the naming of the artist largely a matter of speculation. Of the known hobby-horse artists the most famous was undoubtedly George Cruikshank, who "left an everlasting hoard for all ages to delight in"[153]. However, his input in terms of hobby-horse prints would appear to have been rather less than that of his elder brother Isaac Robert Cruikshank (known as Robert). The illustrated *Stop him who can!!* lithographic print of Denis Johnson (see Fig. 10) is, according to Dorothy George, possibly by or after G. Cruikshank.

---

[153] John Wardroper in *Cruikshank 200*.

The hobby-horse prints

Fig. 97. 'Hobby-Horse Fair' (1819 print, courtesy of Lewis Walpole Library). Robert Cruikshank presents a fascinating 'world upon wheels'. Was there indeed a 'Pilentum coach' (with "the door behind"), as depicted at top left, bottom left and bottom right?

173

A collaboration between Robert Cruikshank and the London publisher G. Humphrey gave rise to no less than five late prints with 'Hobby-Horse Fair' or 'Hobby Fair' in the title. As with the two Tegg prints *Every One His Hobby* (see Figs. 82 and Fig. 83), these amusingly depict a large number of imaginary machines. Two are of particular interest – both slightly confusingly entitled *Hobby-Horse Fair* – one being dated 12th August and the other 10th September 1819. Both prints contain a mixture of real and imaginary items, the earlier one (see Fig. 97) depicting a Pilentum and a Velocimanipede (the second machine in the first line and the fifth in the third line), as well as showing (in the fourth line) what a 'Hobby-Horse Fair' was supposed to look like. *Horse* fairs had of course been held for centuries, and it seems reasonable to assume that a *hobby-horse* fair was a Cruikshank invention never in fact actualized – although we cannot of course be categoric, and no doubt had the velocipede in its various forms continued to be popular beyond the year 1819 such an event could well have taken place. In the late Nineteenth century annual bicycle shows (notably the Stanley Show) were very popular.

There are no known hobby-horse illustrations by that other famous artist of the period Thomas Rowlandson (though a number of modern cycle historians wrongly refer to him as one of the hobby-horse artists). Henry Alken was "one of the most prolific sporting painters and illustrators of his time"[154], but only *Johnson's Pedestrian Hobbyhorse Riding School* has been ascribed to him. William Heath may (according to George) have been responsible for the largest number of prints, although so far as the author is aware only one actually bears his monogram. The only other individuals known to have produced any significant output of hobby-horse drawings are J.L. Marks, C. Williams and the mysterious 'Yedis', possibly Sidebethem.

---

[154] According to *The Oxford Companion to Art*.

Chapter 12
Other velocipedes of the period

Denis Johnson acknowledged his debt to "a certain Foreigner residing abroad", and a contemporary newspaper commented that "the rage for inventions of this sort appears to be travelling from one end of Europe to the other". In England the Johnson velocipede acted as a catalyst to inventors up and down the country, who produced a wide variety of machines. We have already noticed in Chapter 10 a few made specifically or primarily for ladies. The majority of machines may have been little more than prototypes (some may never have been made at all), but a few were certainly produced commercially.

Probably the earliest English machine at this period was the illustrated 'British Facilitator, or Travelling Car', which according to an article in the *Imperial Magazine*[155] was "Invented by B. Smythe, Surveyor, Liverpool, January 25th, 1819". If the January date is correct, it seems unlikely that Johnson's much simpler machine patented only a month before was the inspiration for the Smythe vehicle. Could it be that he named it the *British* Facilitator to distinguish it from the von Drais inventions, or from some other carriage without horses which had appeared abroad?

Whatever the reason for its name, Smythe's brain-child was a remarkable machine. It was operated by "treaders, upon which the

---
[155] 31st May 1819.

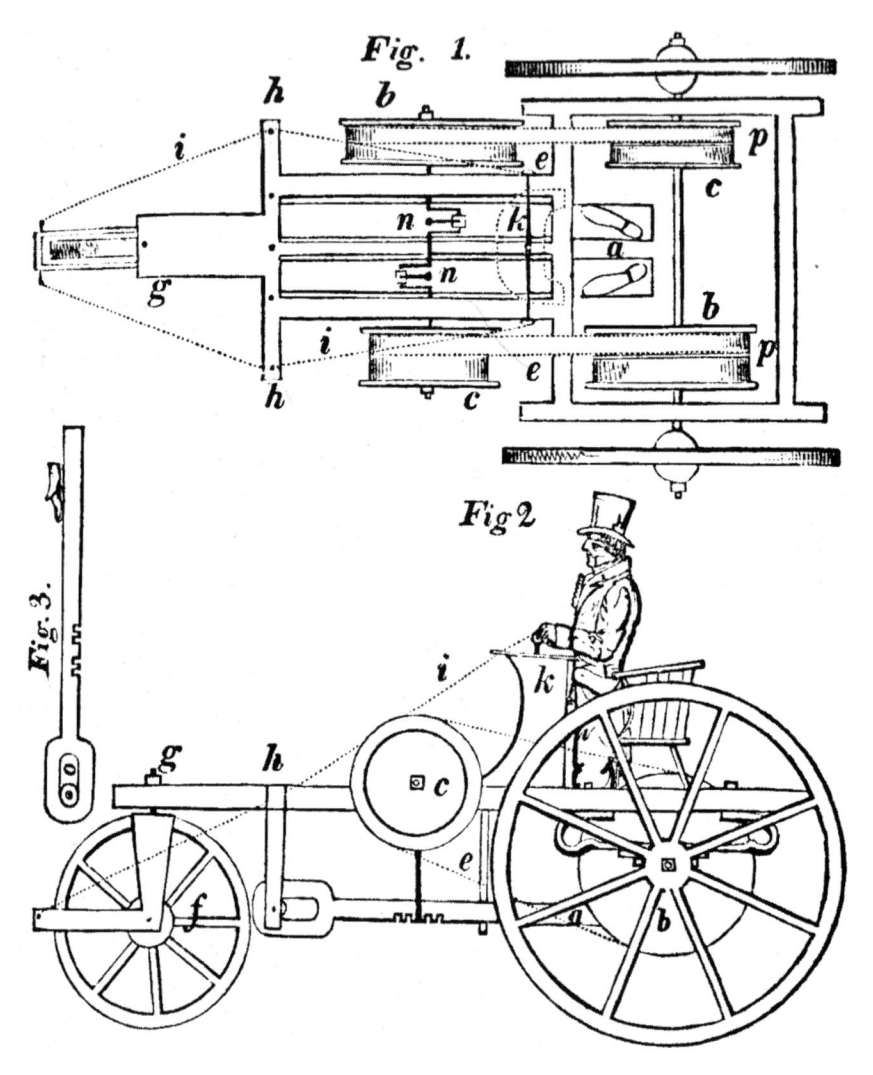

Fig. 98.   British Facilitator, or Travelling Car (Imperial Magazine, May 1819, courtesy of British Library). It appears that, if both the rear drum wheels were thrown out of gear, the rider could free-wheel when going downhill – possibly a dangerous manoeuvre!

whole weight of the body and the strength of the knees are exerted". The action of the "treaders" caused cranks to revolve and turn the two forward drum wheels. These were connected to the two rear drum wheels by straps, so turning the rear axle and driving the back wheels.

What is most surprising however is that, in the early morning of cycle technology in this country, Smythe's 'Travelling Car' (to use its alternative name) had a gear-changing device incorporated. The rider could choose to drive either of the rear wheels, one being geared high and the other low for hill work. The earliest other reference to such a device of which the author is aware is that used by W.H. James in his steam carriage patented in August 1832[156].

Another intriguing early machine was apparently made by "a very ingenious person" of Yarmouth. A report appears in the *Norwich Mercury and Yarmouth, Lynn and Ipswich Herald*[157] in the following terms:

> The Accelerator, or Walking Machine, is the general topic of conversation in this town. Two have been manufactured here, differing slightly from Johnson's machine, and used every morning during the week … but if we are rightly informed, it will soon be superseded by one which is now making [*sic*] by a very ingenious person here, after the manner of the razor-grinding wheel – to be worked by a treadle for both feet. If it succeeds it is expected it will move at the rapid rate of 12 miles an hour.

The puzzling words are those which tell us that the new machine is made "after the manner of the razor-grinding wheel – to be worked by a treadle for both feet". The razor-grinding wheel at this time was operated by a hand crank, as shown in the illustrated 1802 print *Grinders*. This suggests that the Yarmouth machine was driven by cranks attached to the hub of the front wheel, worked by foot pedals

---

[156] Referred to in *The World on Wheels* by H.O. Duncan, Paris, 1926.
[157] 20th March 1819, under the 'Yarmouth' column.

Dashing Dandies

Fig. 99. 'Grinders' (1802 print, lower and upper parts, author's collection). Both one and two crank-handle machines are depicted.

178

(in the Nineteenth century the word 'treadle' was sometimes used where we would now refer to a 'pedal'). If this is correct, we have the prototype of a machine which was not to reappear in this country (imported from France) for something like half-a-century, when it became commonly known as the 'boneshaker'. We can only speculate as to why nothing more was heard of the Yarmouth machine, which would not appear to have been in breach of the Johnson patent.

For the sake of completeness, a brief reference should perhaps be made to one of cycling history's many myths. This is that one of the 1819 prints (*R***L HOBBY's!!!* – see Fig. 100) shows the Prince Regent recumbent on an elongated hobby-horse and being 'ridden' by his supposed mistress Lady Hertford. The prince supports himself by hand rests attached to the front wheel hub, which several commentators have suggested are cranks and pedals. Whatever the status of the Yarmouth machine, this theory is clearly untenable, as has been demonstrated by the well-known cycle historian Derek Roberts,[158] as well as by the French cycle historian Jacques Seray[159].

Another active maker (though not patentee) of velocipedes in 1819 was Charles Lucas Birch, to whom reference has already been made. Like Denis Johnson he was a coachmaker working in the Long Acre area (his actual address being in Great Queen Street, a road which was and is virtually a continuation of Long Acre on the other side of Drury Lane). As has already been noted, there were medical objections to the use of the hobby-horse. According to the *Monthly Magazine*, these objections "led Mr. Birch to apply a simple arrangement of machinery with which to turn the wheels by the actions of the hands or feet"[160]. This was presumably his well-publicised 'Velocimanipede or Lady's Hobby' described in Chapter 10.

---

[158] Roberts, D. *Cycling History, Myths and Queries*, 1991.
[159] In an article in the spring 1997 issue of *The Boneshaker*.
[160] *Monthly Magazine*, November 1819.

Dashing Dandies

Fig. 100. 'R***L HOBBY's!!!' (1819 print, courtesy of British Museum). Both the Prince Regent and Lady Hertford make suggestive comments.

180

Other velocipedes of the period

THE MANIVELOCITER.

THE BIVECTOR.

Fig. 101.   Manivelociter and Bivector (Monthly Magazine, November 1819, courtesy of British Library). Two of Mr. Birch's range of manumotive 'Carriages for Conveyance without Horses'. "The muscular and bodily action is like that of rowing, but far more easy".

Dashing Dandies

But Charles Lucas Birch did not rest on his laurels. After his Velocimanipede had been launched he worked on three further machines (see Figs. 101 and 102). An advert in the *Morning Post* for 15th September 1819 proclaims:

> C.L. Birch has the honour to inform the Nobility, Gentry and Public, that he has invented a machine called the Trivector, which travels without horses: it has been to Brighton in seven hours. To be seen with his Velocimanipede, Manivelociter, and Bivector, at Spring Gardens, from Ten in the Morning till Dusk in the Evening.

THE TRIVECTOR.

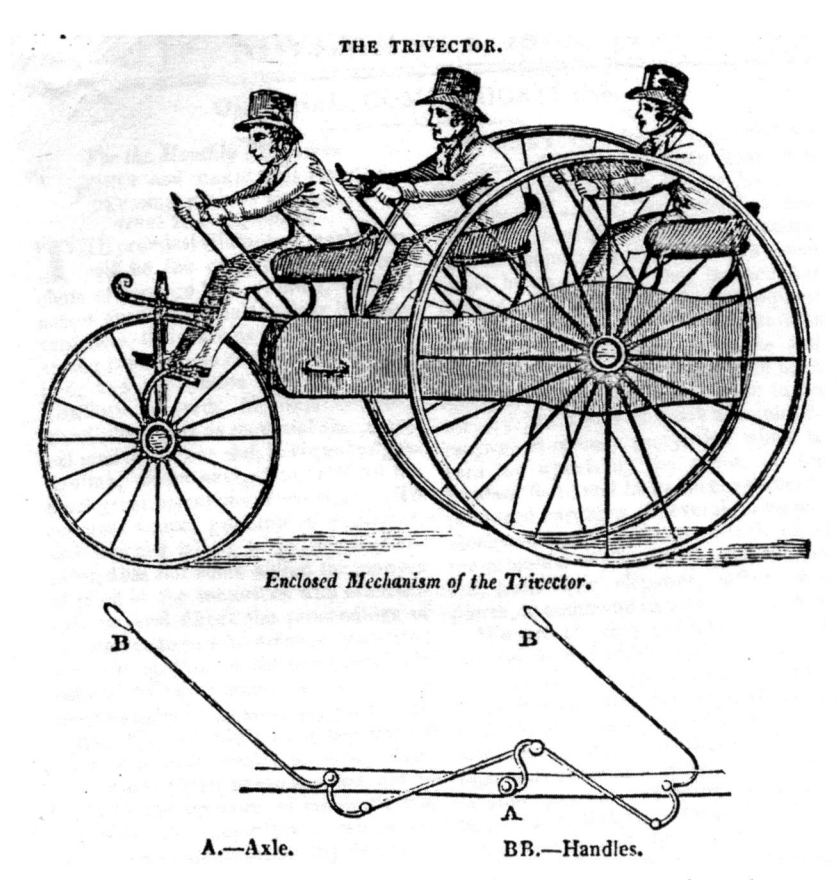

Enclosed Mechanism of the Trivector.

A.—Axle.   BB.—Handles.

Fig. 102. Trivector (Monthly Magazine, November 1819, courtesy of British Library). Another of Mr. Birch's machines.

Admittance One Shilling. Orders received at 71 Great Queen Street, Lincolns Inn Fields[161].

All three new inventions abandon entirely the use of the feet pushing on the ground (retained in the Velocimanipede) in favour of a hand-propelled lever action, as shown in the illustrations from the *Monthly Magazine* article. In the simplest version (the Manivelociter) it must surely have been difficult to obtain any real speed, particularly with a passenger on board, but the tandem and triplet varieties would have been more efficient. The Trivector's voyage to Brighton was reported in the *Monthly Magazine* as follows: "This *Trivector* went from London to Brighton, on Saturday, Sept. 11, worked by three men, as represented in the engraving, in seven hours, where they dined; after which they proceeded thirteen miles further; making together a distance of sixty-seven miles within the day. It would, however, be possible to run this machine 120 miles in the day, without distressing the men".

A writer in the previous month's issue of the *Monthly Magazine*, after referring with approval to the manumotive principle, adds: "Mr. Birch, who has succeeded in this new application, may soon be expected to work his levers, not only by the hand, but by STEAM! Indeed, there can be little doubt but this triumph of mechanics will be effected within the ensuing winter, as we have heard of a patent for securing a new French invention, by which fuel may be economized after the rate of one to ten"[162]. Perhaps a slightly later example of such a machine would be the Londoner Walter Hancock's 'Phaeton' steam three-wheeler of 1829, which it seems travelled hundreds of miles on experimental trips[163].

With the wisdom of hindsight it is easy enough to see that Birch's three September 1819 machines relied too heavily on manumotive

---
[161] *Monthly Magazine*,
[162] *Monthly Magazine*,
[163] According to Duncan in *The World on Wheels*.

Fig 103. Steam velocipedes (author's collection). Probably late 1820s. An amusing little scrap.

action, and as such were bound to remain outside the main stream of velocipede development (in the strict etymological sense they were not 'velocipedes' at all). They were nevertheless viewed as in some respects superior to the Johnson hobby-horse, the author of the *Monthly Magazine* article describing them as having "elegance safety and power" and concluding "we view them as the germs of great social improvements; and amongst other results, we anticipate in them a means of realizing the important design lately proposed by Mr. Burgess, for accelerating the circulation of letters by post".

It was not only Mr. Birch who realized that something had to be done to ease the jarring and even rupturing effect of the Johnson velocipede. A letter from 'E.B.' in the July 1819 issue of the *Monthly Magazine* suggests a simple solution: "I think we have, in a great degree, got rid of jolting, by means of a spring of lance-wood lying along the whole length of the perch, which promises to answer well, with very little increase of weight" (lancewood is known for its tough but elastic quality). As previously noted, the Strangers Hall, Norwich, hobby-horse (see Fig. 41) has the seat attached to a metal spring above the backbone, as does the illustrated machine in the Ipswich Museum store (see Fig. 31). And the hobby-horses

Other velocipedes of the period

Fig. 104. Hobby-horse with suspension spring (Hufstetler collection). Reputedly made and ridden by William Plenty, a carpenter of North Wootton, near Wells.

originally belonging to the Earl of Eglinton in Scotland, and the Duke of Leinster and John Talbot Power in Ireland, all have impressive seat springs.

The illustrated machine now in the Hufstetler collection (see Fig. 104), was for most of the last century at the Wells Museum in Somerset. Its most interesting feature is the suspension spring above the front wheel – another attempt to improve the hobby-horse rider's comfort.

In August 1819 the *Literary Panorama* reports: "A *velocipede*, on a new construction, is said to be building [sic] by an artist at Hereford. It is said to have beams or bodies on springs, and four wheels, which will ensure its safety. It is to quarter on the roads like other carriages, and, with four impellers, it is supposed that it will proceed with astonishing rapidity; but its peculiar recommendation is to be, the conveyance of ladies and two propellers, at the rate of six miles an hour". The 'impellers' or 'propellers' were the gentlemen who were to provide the motive power, though how they were to achieve this is not explained.

Another multi-wheeled machine, this time a three-wheeler, had already been devised further south. It is described even more enigmatically in the *Salisbury and Winchester Journal*: "The hobby-horse has at length made its appearance in Exeter, and is now exhibiting in the playground of the Exeter Grammar School. A gentleman of that city has succeeded in forming a machine with three wheels, with which he travelled on Friday evening, upon the first attempt, upwards of four miles in half an hour"[164]. Further excursions of the speedy three-wheeler are described in *Woolmer's Plymouth & Exeter Gazette*[165].

We know that Johnson's son was active in promoting the 'Velocipede, or Pedestrian Curricle' in Birmingham in the spring of 1819. No doubt this was a source of inspiration for William Field, whose trade card (Birmingham City Library) describes him as a 'Manufacturer of plated Bridle Bitts & Stirrups, Coach & Harness Furniture etc.'.

The following advertisement appears in *Aris's Birmingham Gazette* for 27th September 1819:

VELOCIPEDES

W. FIELD respectfully informs the Gentlemen of Birmingham and its Vicinity, that he has now on sale a Variety of Velocipedes or Walking Machines, upon an improved Principle, which he can recommend for Swiftness and Durability, and on Trial will be found very amusing Exercise and conducive to Health. May be viewed at his Manufactory, Mary Ann Street, St. Paul's, Birmingham. N.B. Price five Guineas. – Gentlemen at a Distance, by inclosing

---

[164] 5th April, 1819.
[165] 3rd and 24th April 1819.

the Amount, may depend upon having their Orders punctually delivered to any Carrier they will please to name. Admittance to practice, 6d. each.

Jim McGurn suggests that these machines were "presumably made under licence from Johnson"[166]. This is unlikely to have been the case, as Field's velocipedes were being advertised after the Johnson hobby-horse craze was largely over, and the Birmingham manufacturer refers to his machines as being "upon an improved Principle". Quite what this was we can now only guess, but the reference to them as 'Walking Machines' suggests that, unlike the Birch velocipedes, they did not have manumotive drive. Interestingly, Field's advertisement is directed solely to the 'Gentlemen of Birmingham and its Vicinity' – the *ladies* of Birmingham are completely ignored.

Rather more detail is supplied in respect of another machine, apparently made in some numbers. The source is *Norfolk Annals* (1901) by Charles Mackie, a work compiled from the files of the *Norfolk Chronicle*. An entry for 5th June 1819 reads:

> Flying Actaeons were exhibited at the Prussia Gardens, Norwich, by Messrs. Brously and Stratford. The machine consists of a chair fixed on a four-wheeled carriage, in which the rider sits and guides the four wheels, turning corners in a similar manner to the velocipedes. One hand only, however, is necessary, the other being at liberty to hold an umbrella. The hind wheels, which force the machine along, are put in motion with the feet of the rider by means of two foot-boards moved up and down alternately. With the assistance of the hand bars in going up steep hills this carriage will travel at the rate of eight miles an hour, and may easily be made for two persons to sit abreast, It is equally convenient for both males and females.

Apart from Johnson's 'pedestrian curricle', the only other velocipede to be patented in 1819 was the 'land punt' (as it has since been

---

[166] *On your Bicycle*, 1st edition, page 22.

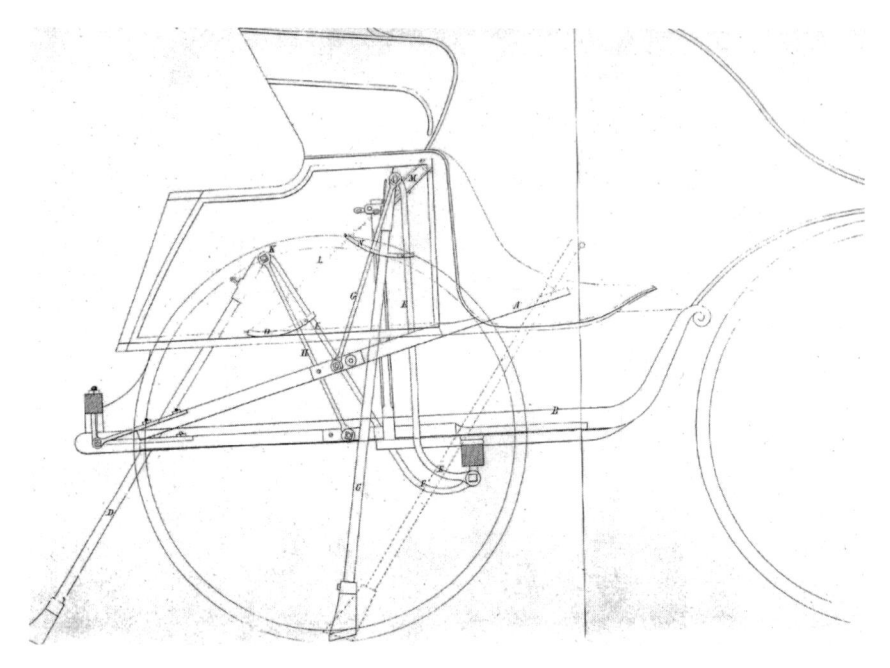

Fig. 105. John Baynes' 'land punt' (patent drawing). "Machinery to be attached to carriages for giving them motion by manual labour or other suitable power". The idea of replacing human by mechanical feet on the ground was ingenious, but probably impractical.

called) of John Baynes, a 'Working Cutler' of Leeds[167]. The way in which this machine worked is reasonably clear from the illustrated patent drawing. The seated rider steered by means of a 'Bath chair' type handle to the front wheel, propelling his carriage forward by long foot treadles, which by means of connecting rods drove "legs or crutches, which bear against the ground as fulcrums, by which the carriage is moved forward", the treadles operating alternately. It is not known whether such a machine was ever actually made, certainly there is no evidence of it coming into widespread use. Interestingly, one of the sketches in the illustrated August 1819 print *Hobby-Horse*

---

[167] Patent no. 4389, 27th September 1819.

Fair (see Fig. 97) is of a dandy propelling a three-wheeled hobby-horse with the aid of hand-held crutches pushing on the ground. As can be seen, steering is intended to be by means of a Bath chair type lever controlled by the rider's head!

An equally strange machine was Sievier's 'Patent Pedestrian Carriage', shown in the illustrated print (Fig. 106) engraved by Williams. This is undated but seems to be a product of the hobby-horse era. It is somewhat reminiscent of a two-wheeler of the 1880s known popularly (if not officially) then and now as the 'Otto Dicycle' – the important distinction being that the later item was driven by pedals.

The author has come across no other reference to Sievier's machine apart from this print. However, the article was obviously made in some numbers as the print legend states: "Manufactured and Sold by LEES COTTAM & HALLEN at their Repository Winsley Street opposite the Pantheon Oxford Street Steel Yard Wharf, Upper Thames Street and at their Manufactory, Cornwall Road, Surrey side of Waterloo Bridge". A presumably contemporary handwritten comment on this particular copy of the print states "Exhibiting at the Great Rooms, Spring Gardens". Lees, Cottam and Hallen were advertising a wide range of items (though not at this stage the Sievier machine) in the *Salisbury and Winchester Journal* in the early months of 1819.

The carriage is said to be "for Ladies & Gentlemen". There would appear to be an important difference between the types provided for each sex. The lady has a seat seemingly suspended from the axle the use of which would no doubt considerably reduce the efficacy of foot propulsion. As in the case of the much later 'Otto Dicycle', a 'tip-tail' is provided to prevent the lady from falling over backwards. The gentleman's version would seem to be rather different in that he is shown apparently standing, not sitting, between the two large wheels. It may be that there was some sort of saddle or sling

Dashing Dandies

Fig. 106. 'Sievier's Patent Pedestrian Carriage' (c.1820 print, courtesy of Lorne Shields). The progenitor of the two-track, two-wheel velocipede which was to reach its apotheosis some sixty years later.

190

suspended from the axle, enabling the rider to take the weight of his body off the ground, leaving his feet free to propel the wheels by pushing forward along the path in hobby-horse fashion, but this is far from clear. It is also not apparent how the vehicle was steered. No doubt we shall have a much better idea of exactly how it operated if and when the patent is discovered. Searches of the British, French and American patent record over a large number of years have so far produced no result.

The Sievier pedestrian carriage print legend claims: "The superiority and safety of this machine above all those before invented is immediately discovered upon the least attention to its mechanic properties. A mile has been performed in less than 3 minutes and twelve miles within the hour. It is particularly well adapted for Gentlemen's pleasure grounds, or persons whose occupation in the Country requires a large quantity of ground to be gone over". The claim that the machine could travel at more than 20 m.p.h. over a measured mile is certainly an astonishing one.

Remarkably similar to the Sievier machine is one described in the *Gentleman's Magazine* for June 1819 (and elsewhere) as follows:

> PEDESTRIAN CHARIOT. Mr. Howell, of Bristol, has invented a machine, of infinitely greater power and utility than the Velocipede. Its chief attractions are its simplicity, being eligible for the conveyance of ladies, and even children. The wheels, which are upwards of six feet in diameter, run parallel to each other; and as the seat is below the centre of gravity, the rider can neither be thrown, nor easily lose his equilibrium. From the increased circumference of the wheel, and the consequently decreased friction of the axle, a greater degree of velocity may be given, with a considerably diminished impetus; and this renders it of much greater facility of management, either on the level road or the most rapid descent. The machine may be constructed to carry two or three persons, with a portmanteau or other luggage.

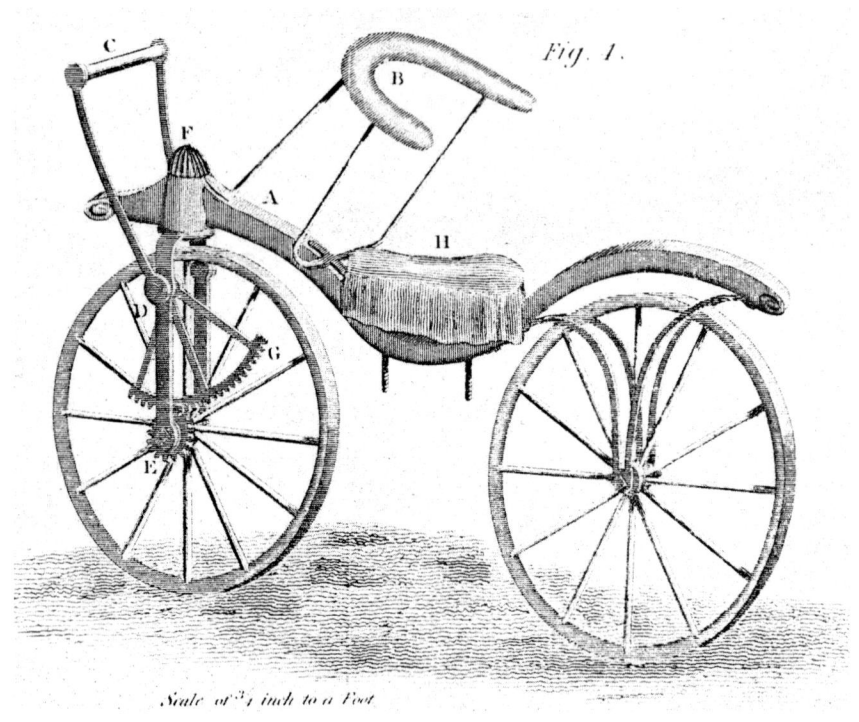

Fig. 107.   Gompertz's modified velocipede ('The Repertory of Arts', 1821). The first two-wheeler which envisaged the possibility of the rider's feet being kept off the ground for an extended period. However, unlike the Johnson machine, no foot rests appear to have been provided or allowed for.

It would appear from an item in the *Liverpool Mercury*[168] that Mr. Howell's machine was known as a Gymnasidromist (the Regency gentlemen seem to have had a penchant for long and supposedly impressive names for their inventions). In another newspaper item briefly referring to the machine we are told that "it is at present exhibiting in London". Howell's two-wheeler was also known as a Patent Equestrian Chariot, and (more accurately) as a Patent Pedestrian Chariot[169]. It may be that, in the case of both the Sievier and Howell

---

[168]   28th May 1819.
[169]   Bristol papers, May 1819.

machines, the term 'patent' was used loosely to describe a supposedly original invention, even though no formal patent was obtained.

A brief reference has already been made to Lewis Gompertz of Kennington, who emphasized how short was the heyday of the ordinary hobby-horse velocipede. He himself made a valiant effort to revive its fortunes by an invention which provided an additional method of propulsion to the simple expedient of pushing with the feet on the ground. The illustration from *The Repertory of Arts*[170] shows how Gompertz modified the velocipede by the addition of a rack-and-pinion mechanism.

Strangely, although Gompertz's illustration is clearly a modified Johnson machine, he gives no credit to the London coachmaker, referring only to "that ingenious and well-known invention, the velocipede, of Baron von Dray". Perhaps he was nervous of inviting a claim that his machine was in breach of the Johnson patent.

Gompertz describes the use of his machine as follows: "The chief object is to bring the arms of the rider into action, in assistance to his legs, and consists in the application of a handle C, which is to be worked backwards and forwards, to which is attached a circular rack DG, which works in a pinion E, with a ratch wheel on the front wheel of the velocipede, and which, on being *pulled* by the rider with both hands, propels the machine forwards, and when thrust from him (in order to repeat the stroke) does not send it back again, on account of the ratch which allows the pinion to turn in that direction free of the wheel". Gompertz envisages the possibility of his two-wheeler being driven by the arms alone with the rider's feet off the ground "if the ground be good and if he can balance himself".

Gompertz was it seems closely involved in 1824 with the foundation of the Society for the Prevention of Cruelty to Animals (now the RSPCA). The suggestion has been made by Les Bowerman that

---

[170] Volume 39, 2nd Series, 1821.

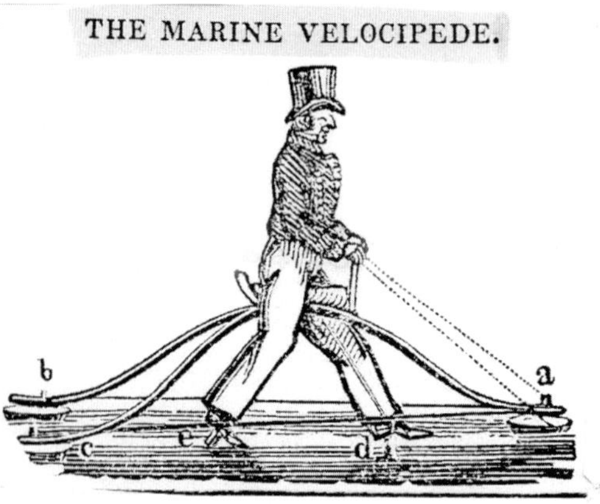

THE MARINE VELOCIPEDE.

Fig. 108. Kent's Marine Velocipede. It was said to have "excited a degree of interest scarcely warranted by any practical utility likely to arise from its adoption".

Gompertz's interest in the velocipede would have stemmed from the fact that he was anxious to encourage a substitute for the horse-drawn vehicle of his day. However, it is likely that at most only a few of his machines were made. It appears one was displayed as a historical item at the Stanley Show (the late-Nineteenth century equivalent of today's Motor Show) as late as 1881, possibly lent by the Polytechnic Institution.

One of the earliest of a number of Nineteenth century water cycles was the illustrated 'Marine Velocipede' of a Mr. Kent of Glasgow, described in *The Kaleidoscope* of 24th July 1821 (see Fig. 108). The invention had been widely criticized as being of clumsy construction, as a result of which Mr. Kent was "engaged in simplifying and reducing the bulk of his apparatus". However, another report 'Walking upon Water'[171] informs us: "A few days since, Mr. Kent walked on the Monkland Canal, at the rate of three miles in the hour, which was witnessed by about 200 persons".[172]

The story is continued two years later in John Badcock's 1823 book *Domestic Amusements, or Philosophical Recreations*, where we learn of

---

[171] *The National Gazette and Literary Register*, Philadephia, 12th June 1821.
[172] The Monkland Canal ran from Monklands to Glasgow, but was abandoned for navigation in 1942.

'The Aquatic Tripod, or Tricipede'. As can be seen in the illustrated print from the book (Fig. 109), this seems to be a development of Kent's machine rather than a new invention, as no other inventor's name is provided and the item "varies in some trifling points in the hands of several makers". We are told that the machine "has been lately used on some waters of Lincolnshire, with complete success".

And the *London Journal of Arts and Sciences* for 1822 contains the following interesting item[173]:

> A New Velocipede Has been exhibited in various parts of the metropolis during the month of September, which promises to be of positive utility. Its inventor is a shoemaker, a native of Newark-on-Trent, in Nottinghamshire, but whose name we have not yet been able to obtain. The machine consists of three wheels; one behind, about three feet in diameter, over which the inventor sits; and two lower ones before. It is worked by the hands, with two short handles, (without apparently any great exertion), which set two wheels in motion; these operate upon two levers, which set the machine going at the rate of six miles or more per hour. It is by far the most complete apparatus of the kind which has been yet invented, and must become, we think, a really useful vehicle. The inventor has travelled in fine weather with it sixty miles a day. He has two iron stirrups, in which he places his feet; they keep him steady on the seat. We have ourselves seen the vehicle in operation. The ease with which it is impelled and turned round in every direction is admirable. We shall endeavour to procure a drawing of it for a future number of our Journal and we hope that the inventor himself will not be forgotten by a liberal and intelligent public.

Unfortunately, a search over the following two years did not disclose a drawing, and a similar report in *The Times* newspaper was likewise unillustrated. But in any event, so far as commercially successful machines are concerned, Denis Johnson's foot-propelled two-wheeler clearly remains in a class of its own.

---

[173] Page 199, vol.4, 1st series.

Dashing Dandies

Fig. 109. The Aquatic Tripod, or Tricipede (courtesy of Lorne Shields). Apparently, this machine was utilized with success during the entire winter of 1822.

196

Appendix

John Fairburn's 'New Pedestrian Carriage' booklet

Fairburn's Edition.

AN
ACCURATE, WHIMSICAL, AND SATIRICAL,
DESCRIPTION
OF THE NEW
PEDESTRIAN CARRIAGE,
OR
Walking Accelerator!!
INCLUDING
A COLOURED CARICATURE.

Price Six-pence.

Appendix

FAIRBURN'S
WHIMSICAL DESCIRPTION
OF THE NEW
PEDESTRIAN CARRIAGE,
OR,
Dandy Hobby-Horse.
INCLUDING
A SATIRICAL ACCOUNT
OF
A RACE FROM ALPHA COTTAGE TO TYBURN,
BETWEEN THE TWO NOBLE LORDS
Whiskerandos and Smoothchops.
WITH SOME ACCOUNT OF A NEW MILITARY CORPS ABOUT TO BE RAISED,
CALLED,
The Regent's Pedestrio Equestria Chargers,
TO BE COMMANDED BY
TOM CHIFFNEY, Jun.
AND STATIONED ON THE STEYNE.
AND OF THE
Anti-Straddling Chargers,
FOR THE USE OF
THE DANDIZETTES.

Mount, Dandies, mount, and roll along,
Subjects of satire, mirth, and song;
Grease as you like the Hobby's wheels,
Fairburn will still stick to your heels,
And wield his lash of playful satire,
O'er all who over-step Dame Nature.

Embellished with a Caricature Frontispiece.

LONDON:
PRINTED AND PUBLISHED BY JOHN FAIRBURN, 2, BROADWAY,
LUDGATE-HILL.

Appendix

ACCURATE DESCRIPTION

OF THE NEW

New Pedestrian Carriage,

&c. &c.

IN the Frontispiece to this work is a Correct Representation of the Pedestrian Carriage, or Walking Accelerator, drawn by an eminent Artist, from one of the latest improvements of the Machine. It was originally the invention of an ingenious German, Baron Charles de Drais, but has been introduced into this country and improved by Mr. Johnson, coachmaker in Long Acre, who has secured it by taking out Letters Patent. The Machine is of the most simple kind, supported by two light wheels running on the same line; the front wheel turning on a pivot, which, by means of short lever, gives the direction in turning it to one side or the other, the hind wheel always running in one direction. The rider mounts it, and seats himself in a saddle conveniently fixed on the back of the horse, (if allowed to be calle so,) and placed in the middle between the wheels, the feet are placed flat on the ground, so that in the first step to give the Machine motion the heel should be the first part of the foot to touch the ground, and so on with the other foot alternately, as if walking, observing always to begin the movement very gently. In the front,

6

before the rider, is placed a cushion, to rest the arms on, while the hands hold the lever: this cushion should be properly called a balance, as it answers that purpose; for in giving a short turn, if the Machine inclines to the left, the right arm is pressed on the balance, which brings the Machine upright again, and so *vice versa*.

A person thus mounted, and propelling himself, appears to be skaiting, which the motion of the feet greatly resembles. It is evident, that the whole weight of the body being relieved from the limbs, an immense portion of fatigue must be saved; and as a slight impulse produces a considerable effect upon a Machine so constructed, a velocity is attained far beyond what the utmost personal exertion, unassisted by art, can accomplish.

Experiments have shown that it is easy to travel fifty or more miles a day on these " German Horses;" and as a riding-school is about to be opened for them, we expect to see them brought into extensive use. For exercise in parks, &c. they seem to be admirably adapted; and from a trial of their powers, we can say that their management is very readily acquired.

It is stated that a person well practised, can travel eight, nine, and even ten miles an hour, on good and level ground; and that the Accelerator has even beat the Brighton four-horse coach by half an hour.

Mr. Johnson's Repository is daily thronged with visitors, and it is amusing to see his servant riding about a long room to *show the Horse*, threading the carriages, and wheeling and turning with great precision. They may also be seen in a large Exhibition-room, near Exeter-Change, Strand; and at another in Brewer-street, Gold-

7

en-square; which have been engaged for that purpose. The cost is about Eight Guineas.

The following account of the Machine is given by the inventor, Baron Charles de Drais, master of the woods and forests of H. R. H. *the Grand Duke of Baden.*

1. That on a well-maintained post road, it will travel up hill as fast as an active man can walk.

2. On a plain, even after a heavy rain, it will go six or seven miles an hour, which is as swift as a courier.

3. When roads are dry and firm, it runs on a plain at the rate of eight or nine miles an hour, which is equal to a horse's gallop.

4. On a descent, it equals a horse at full speed.

Its theory is founded on the application of a wheel to the action of a man in walking. With respect to the economy of power, this invention may be compared to that very antient one of carriages. As a horse draws, in a well-constructed carriage, both the carriage and its load much easier than he could carry the load alone on his back; so a man conducts, by means of the Accelerator, his body easier than if he had its whole weight to support on his feet. It is equally incontestible, that the Accelerator, as it makes but one impression, or rut, may always be directed on the best part of a road. On a hard road, the rapidity of the Accelerator resembles that of an expert skaiter; as the principles of the two motions are the same. In truth, it runs a considerable distance while the rider is inactive, and with the

8

same rapidity as when his feet are in motion; and, in a descent, it will beat the best horses in a great distance, without being exposed to the risks incidental to them, as it is guided by the mere gradual motion of the fingers, and may be instantly stopped by the feet.

It consists of two wheels, one behind the other, connected by a perch, on which a saddle is placed, for the seat of the traveller. The front wheel is made to turn on a pivot, and is guided in the same manner as a Bath chair. On a cushion in front the arms are rested; and by this means the instrument and traveller are kept in equilibrio.

ITS MANAGEMENT.

The traveller having placed himself in the position represented in the plate, his elbows extended, and his body inclined a little forward, must place his arms on the cushion, and preserve his equilibrium by pressing lightly on that side which appears to be rising. The rudder (if it may be so called) must be held by both hands, which are not to rest on the cushion, that they may be at full liberty, as they are as essential to the conduct of the machine as the arms are to the maintenance of the balance of it (attention will soon produce sufficient dexterity for this purpose): then, placing the feet lightly on the ground, long but very slow steps are to be taken, in a right line, at first; taking care to avoid turning the toes out, lest the heels should come in contact with the hind wheel. It is only after having acquired dexterity in the equilibrium and direction of the Accelerator, that the attempt to increase the motion

9

of the feet, or to keep them elevated while it is in rapid motion, ought to be attempted.

The saddle may be raised or lowered, as well as the cushion, at pleasure; and thus suited to the height of various persons.

The inventor proposes to construct them to carry two persons, and to be impelled by each alternately, or both at once; and also with three or four wheels, with a seat for a lady: besides the application of a parasol or umbrella, he also proposes to avail himself of a sail, with a favourable wind.

This instrument appears to have satisfied a desideratum in mechanics: all former attempts have failed, upon the known principle that power is obtainable only at the expense of velocity. But the impelling principle is totally different from all others: it is not derived from the body of the machine, but from a resistance operating externally, and in a manner most conformable to nature—the resistance of the feet upon the ground. The body is carried and supported, as it were, by two skates, while the impulse is given by the alternate motion of both the legs. The Germans call this machine " Drais Laufmashin," and the French " Draisena."

Under the direction of Baron Drais, a carriage was some years since constructed to go without horses; but as it required two servants to work it, and was a very complicated piece of workmanship, besides being heavy and expensive, the Baron, after having brought it to some degree of perfection, relinquished the design altogether in favour of the present machine.

B

10
WHIMSICAL ANECDOTES.

This new invented charger is, in all probability, a revived descendant of the celebrated Trojan horse, being formed of wood, but, in point of animation or soul, it is nearly upon a par with the nondescripts which bestride it, vulgarly y'clept Dandies, for to those *beings* the use of it seems at present confined; when the blind lead the blind they often fall into the ditch is a saying verified in this instance, as numerous disasters have befallen the Dandy Race, who, wanting courage and capacity to mount and guide a living animal, have been kindly accommodated with one suitable to their taste and closely allied to their own species. When the Athenian ambassadors waited upon Agesilaus, the warlike king of Sparta, they found him riding on a Hobby-Horse, surrounded by his children. They smiled upon him with contempt. " Friends," said the monarch, " smile not until you have a family of your own: no " man is a hero in his domestic life." He then retired and came forth in his royal robes, astonished them by profound reasoning, and denounced against Athens that war which shook her foundations, and established the independence of Thessaly.

All men have their *Hobby-Horse*. Bonaparte's *Hobby* was *universal dominion*. King Louis's *Hobby* is *gluttony*. Lord Castlereagh's *Hobby* is *taxation*. John Bull's *Hobby* is *grumbling*. And our *royal* gentry's *Hobby* is *women and wine*. Now why should not some of these Dandy *Hobby-Horse*-mounted gentlemen rise from their amusements with all the energy of an Agesilaus, and nobly shine in defence of their country. Alas! no; Agesilaus never rode his *Hobby-Horse* in the field (as they do in the Park); he wore no *stays* but what were made of *steel*. He kept no *rouge-box*, nor wore *gilt spurs*, and " tetes de mutton." Sorry am I that no comparison can be drawn from antient history favourable to the *Dandy*

11

Hussars forming Johnson's *Western Division of Chargers*, for they have not yet passed Temple-bar, when they do, they will be apt to get very roughly handled, if they crack a pane in the *shawl-warehouse*, at the corner of Fleet-street, where the worthy Alderman is as partial to a Dandy as the devil is said to be to holy water; and he who so ably purged the city of wh——s, would, no doubt, take equal pleasure in clearing it of Dandy Rogues.

If we are *literally* to shoot folly as it flies, Hyde-park, on a Sunday would be strewed with dead, and not a Dandy left to tell the tale, like the army of Sennacharib who were slain in one night before the walls of Jerusalem, it might be said, in the language of the antient *Irish Jewish* historian, " *And. lo, when they arose in the morning they were all dead corpses.*" The heel of Achilles was his only vulnerable part; 'tis hard to tell where our Dandy-riders are vulnerable. Their booted ancles and whalebone waists must be bullet-proof; and, I believe, the only way to discomfit them is to upset the *charger* and break the rider's neck; even that would be problematical, on account of the *stuffing*. A Dandy's stock of linen is not large, and they always carry their foul clothes in their neck-cloths. The *pedestrian carriage* is certainly an excellent invention, though it forcibly reminds me of the Irishman who called a chair out of which they knocked the bottom, and, after trudging him through the mud for a mile, opened the door and let him out, when Pat, paying his fare, observed— " By Jasus, now, and if it wasn't for the name of the thing, a fellow might just as well walk."

The fantastic toe and heel is kept in play; and I question but *Johnson's Patent Hobby* will be so useful in giving the first rudiments of dancing, that it will destroy the trade of *Hopkins* and *Walker* in the same way that *Logier* and *Kalkbrenner* have rendered nugatory *Clementi*, and his *Early Instructions for the Piano-Forte*.

12

Out of evil cometh forth good, saith the Psalmist, out of folly cometh wisdom, and a lesson of moral instruction may be derived from the disasters of those Dandies who have presumed to mount this " infernal machine." " My son, seek another kingdom, Macedon is unworthy of thee," said Philip to his heir, Alexander, when he had subdued the spirit of the horse, Bucephalus. *Vice versa* might be applied to the *mounted* Dandy, —" Seek another kingdom, thou art not worthy to remain in this." However, wise men will sometimes indulge in childish amusements from whim, from caprice, or a delight which every mind at times feels to wander back to the Hobby-horsical days of childhood, and muse on joys that never return.

> " Who foremost now delight to cleave
> With pliant arm thy glassy wave,
> The captive linnet which enthral," &c.

Thus wrote Gray in the evening of his days; and with the same amiable retrospective view, I suppose Captain Hoy, a hero reeking from the field of Waterloo mounted one of Johnson's Chargers, (his own, I have no doubt, has his bones whitening in the summer's sun on the bed of honour,) he dash'd up *Long-acre*, and had proceeded as far as Duncombe's, in Little Queen-street, where he curbed the impetuosity of his fiery charger, and stopped to read the bill of Matthews's budget.

> Ah, me! what perils doth environ
> The man who meddles with cold iron.

The bridle of the charger was rudely seized, and, before he could draw his cold iron from its sheath, he was man-handled by some half-dozen men in buckram, and a fellow in a laced hat and shabby blue coat roared—

> " Zounds, I'm the *beadle of the parish*."
> To Marlborough-street, the Captain he drags,
> And swore he would fine him because on the flags
> He had caught him; for he had stuck close to his heels,
> As he rumbled along them his charger's wheels.

13

It was in vain to attempt fighting a cock on his own dunghill, so the Captain bowed to superior force and attended the farce of

THE BEADLE OUTWITTED.

John Kendrick, the beadle, who I am sure has had as many of Mother Cummins's fair and frail disciples in tow, as he has drank glasses of gin at their cost, laid his charge against the captain, who was convicted under the Paving-Act, (and a d——d hard-headed act it is for poor barrow-women and sellers of dogs-meat). He paid his fine of £2, and instanter laid an information against the "Jack in Office," who had imprudently mounted the captain's charger, and rode her through Queen's Court (a paved one) in triumph. The worthy Magistrate, Mr. Farrant, of Marlborough-street-office, convicted him also, and he paid the penalty of £2, amidst the laughter of a crowded office.

Vide Morning Advertiser, 11*th March.*

I love to see the "biter bit," and in this case it is truly so. The fame of Johnson's Walking-Accelerator reached Brighton, and attracted the attention of one, from whose name we may hereafter have them called,

JOHNSON'S ROYAL HOBBY-HORSE CHARGERS.

Four of them have been sent down to the Kremlin, at Brighton; when it was whispered they were on the go, numbers assembled to view this new addition to the royal stud, and addition to the cares of Sir Benjamin Bloomfield and the Duke of Montrose. The Duke, as Master of the Horse, must be a judge of the *new built* animal. Sir Benjamin, as *Comptroller of the Stud-House*, must rub down Johnson's *Patent Charger* to a brilliancy fit to dazzle royal eyes.

When this was known, numbers attended to see the steeds go forth, no Arabians clad in gold coverings, no

14

harnessing of Eastern splendour, no prancing heroic animals appeared. A military waggon received the *wooden carcasses* of four well-painted *Dandy Chargers*, and in all the waggon-train pomp of peaceful military parade, Colonel Jen—k—n trotted off with them as guide and guard on the road to his royal master's pavilion. If the creatures give satisfaction, it is understood to be the royal intention to mount upon them a regiment of Lancers, to be called

THE DANDY PEDESTRIO EQUESTRIA CHARGERS.

They are to be stationed on the Steyne, and assist in conveying the royal household to and from London. Young Chiffney, from the high estimation in which he is held, will probably command *this invulnerable* corps.

As £10,000 per annum is not sufficient to maintain a *prince's horse*, one of *Johnson's Chargers* has been bespoke to convey the royal duke *once a month* to Windsor, and as the animal cannot eat, the expense of *baiting* on the road will be saved.

A penny sav'd is a penny got,
To go to *Mother Carey's* pot.

It is likewise in contemplation to bring those useful machines forward at the theatres. Drury-Lane has been put to great expenses by hiring Astley's horses, that burthen upon the dilapidated treasury is now about to be removed, and Blue Beard will be got up in style, in order to astonish the public with JOHNSON'S HOBBY-HORSES running their wheels over the toes of the elephants.

In fact, in all departments of the state where *Asses* are so generally employed, *Dandy Hobby-Horses* will, in future, be substituted in their places.

15

A RACE FROM ALPHA-COTTAGE TO TYBURN.

A noble Dandy-Race was run for the purpose of trying the bottom and mettle of these dumb animals. The bet was one hundred guineas a side, from the Alpha cottages, on the Edgware-road, to Tyburn-turnpike. At one o'clock Lord Y―――― mounted *Whiskerandos*, and the Earl of B―――― mounted *Smoothchops*. They started at full speed and kept neck and neck until near the *water-works*, when Whiskerandos became restive and ran against a cow: by the help of a chimney-sweep, the *noble rider* preserved his balance, tightened his reins and again dashed forward on the course. At the corner of Connaught-mews *Smoothchops* bolted, but the Earl brought him up in style, by the end of Lady Augusta Murray's Mansion, and pull baker, pull devil, on they drove, helter skelter, and at Tyburn-turnpike *Wiskerandos* gained the heat by half a neck; scarce a ragamuffin in London but had assembled to view the contest and pick pockets; the applauses which they bellowed upon the victory were loud and long, and extended from St. Giles's to Long-Acre, and from thence to Carlton-House, where a *carrier* pigeon conveyed the glorious tidings to Brighton under his wing.

It is hard to tell which of these two nobles merited first to arrive *at Tyburn* and win *by the neck,* but as both did their best, their claims to *be exalted* might be considered as equal.

A Dandy mounted upon one of these chargers, *charged* a watchman in Catharine-street, who instantly knocked him down horse and all, and carried both to the watch-house, where the Dandy and his horse were released after a night's incarceration upon paying " fines and charges," which, with his doctor's bill, (for his head was well scarified,) would amount to full £3 : 10 : 0, the price of *Aske's* best pair of *Dandy stays.*

16

A MOUNTED TAR CAPSIZING A HOST OF CORRUPTION.

A naval officer mounted one of these *chargers* in Pall-Mall, and, as sailor like, no great adepts in riding, he swore he would steer a straight course and run down the devil if he came across his hawse. The black gentleman did not appear to obstruct his course; but running at the rate of *ten knots* an hour, he capsized a Dandy, a Member of Parliament, a Pig, an Apple-woman, a Cabinet Minister, a Prince, a Newfoundland Dog, and a Bishop.

The rapidity with which all this was executed, proves that, under the guidance of *discretion*, these Hobby-Horses may be made very useful in *accelerating* every wise and nobler art of man, and though now only vehicles for carrying baboons and monkeys, may, in time, carry *men* to some purpose; for instance, *soldiers* and *electors* could be conveyed to the hustings quickly and cheaply, and *criminals* to the gallows with the greatest pleasure. There is now constructing a Charger for females of the same nature—wood and paint—for the use of the ladies, it is to be named the

ANTI-STRADDLING CHARGER.

Fairburn, with his usual attention to the public, will, in a few days, present an exact print of it, drawn from the thing itself, by the same artist who has so admirably designed the plate to this little work.

> Mount, Dandies, mount, and roll along,
> Subject of satire, mirth, and song;
> Grease as you like the Hobby's wheels,
> *Fairburn* will still stick to your heels,
> And wield his lash of playful satire,
> Oe'r all who over-step dame Nature.

THE END.

Printed by J. Fairburn, 2, Broadway, Ludgate-Hill.

Index

Allen family:
  Continuation of business
    started by Johnson   62, 63
  Family relationship with
    Johnson   61
  Johnson & Allen partnership   61
Aquatic Tripod, or Tricipede,
  invention of Mr. Kent   195, 196

Barclay, Captain, famous
  pedestrian wager   76
Bath:
  Early use of Laufmaschine   12
  Johnson's tour of England, visit   52
Baynes, John, patentee of 'land
  punt'   187, 188
Berkhampstead Sports,
  banning of dandy horses   87
Beverley, activities of
  Rev. Coltman   110, 111
Birch, Charles Lucas,
  velocipede maker   140, 143, 179,
     181–184
Birmingham:
  Field, William, velocipede
    maker   186, 187
  Johnson exhibiting at   52, 186
Bivector, manumotive
  machine   181–184
Blackheath, proposed racing at   81

Blandford, hobby-horse hoax   73, 74
Boots, metal strengthening for
  riding   66, 69
Brighton:
  four hobby-horses delivered to
    Prince Regent's Brighton
    home   122
  hobby-horses ridden from
    London   122, 123
  Trivector ridden from
    London   182, 183
Bristol:
  Durdham Down,
    hit-and-run rider   83
  Johnson's invitation to the
    ladies   131
  pavement riding of
    hobby-horses banned   86
  start of Johnson's tour of
    England   52
British Facilitator, or Travelling
  Car   175–177

Cambridge, pavement riding
  of hobby-horses banned   86
Canterbury, 'match against
  time', ride to   77
Cheltenham (vicinity of,
  pavement riding of
  hobby-horses banned   86

Children, use of hobby-horses
  by 112, 113
Chingford, hobby-horse race
  between two riders 77
Coleridge, Samuel Taylor,
  hobby-horse rider 107
Coltman, Rev. Joseph, weighty
  hobby-horse rider 110, 111
Commemorative plaque to
  Denis Johnson 17, 18

Dandies:
  character of 101, 102, 104
  conspicuous display
    proposed 105, 106
  Lord Petersham 104, 105
  nursery rhyme 106, 107
  racing incident 104
  reason for hobby-horse
    production 104
Dandy-horse – *see* Hobby-horse
Deptford, dandies race at 104
Donkey, race with hobby-horse
  at Nottingham 82
Draisienne – *see* Laufmaschine
Draisine – *see* Laufmaschine
Drais, Karl von:
  birth and early life 4
  death and erection of
    monument 12
  first use of Laufmaschine in
    Germany 1
  inventor of Fahrmaschine 4, 5
  inventor of Laufmaschine 1
  other inventions 5
  portraits 6, 7
Duke of York:
  acquisition of Johnson
    machine 123
  depiction as hobby-horse
    rider 123, 124

monthly journey to Windsor 123
Enneapheron, machine to
  carry nine persons 137, 139
Exeter:
  the hobby-horse at 186
  three-wheeled machine 186

Fahrmaschine:
  invention by von Drais 4, 5
  reasons for relinquishment 5
Falkirk, tour from London to 65
Farnham, accident to rider at 83
Flying Actaeons, at Norwich 187
Field, William, velocipede
  maker 186. 187
Fob seal depicting hobby-horse
  rider 103
Free wheel, early use by
  Gompertz 193

Gompertz, Lewis,
  inventor of modified
  hobby-horse 92, 193, 194
Goy, 'Athletic Outfitter',
  ownership of dandy horse 98
Grimaldi, Joseph, probable
  pantomime hobby-horse rider 114
Gymnasidromist, term
  employed for Howell's
  machine 192

Hancock & Co., makers of
  Pilentum and Enneapheron 137
Hereford velocipede,
  four-wheeler 185, 186
Hobby-horse:
  Johnson machines:
    brake, absence of 21, 82
    children's machines 26, 28, 29
    colours 30

214

Index

cost 101
dandies as reason for
 production 104
details of surviving
 machines 21–24, 30, 36
earliest known 38
first sold 50
foot rests 36, 38, 40, 41
handle (or handlebar) 33
lady's, with dropped
 frame 131–134
latest known 29, 31
manufacture and marketing 49
materials employed 58
name plate 21, 23
numbering and dating 29, 31
ornamentation 21, 24, 36
patent 18–20 and frontispiece
Royal ownership 122, 123, 128
seat (adjustable) 20
stand for 21
steering, 'direct' or
 indirect' 31, 33, 37–40
three-wheeler 24–26
weight 24
wheels and spokes 21
Miscellaneous:
alternative names 48–49
archetypal bicycle xi (Preface)
commercial production of
 non-Johnson machines 175
contemporary view of
 invention xi (Preface)
details of surviving
 non-Johnson machines 34,
  39, 41, 43–47, 171, 172
frame spring, addition of 185
German origin of machine 1
hoaxes 73–75
'hobby-horse' word
 contrasted with 'velocipede' 49

iron machines 58, 59
non-steerable machines 93–95
poem 'The Velocipede' 74, 75
poem 'The Velocipede' 121, 122
public interest 71, 73
seat spring, addition of 39, 41,
  47, 59, 184, 185
songs 117, 118
sweepstake 50, 51
theatrical interest 114
velocipede, 1822 invention
 of shoemaker 195
watercolour painting of
 hobby-horse riders 158
Use:
accidents 82–85
carrying of mail 65–67
children and youths, by 21, 26,
  28, 29, 100, 112, 113
clergymen, by 65, 109–112
dandies, by 69
decline in, reasons for 90–92
distances ridden 64, 65
early use in London 64
Grimaldi, by, in pantomime 114
hiring 60, 64, 101
Hyde Park 34, 71–73
in Ireland 171, 172
in Scotland 34, 43
instructions for riding 66
ladies, by 129, 131–133,
  140, 143
measuring roads 66
medical implications 64, 91, 92
military (envisaged) 88, 89
Nineteenth century
 generally 93–99
nobility, acquisition and use
 by 34, 119, 121, 122
opposition 150

215

pantomime, first appearance
  on stage in 114
prosecutions for pavement
  riding 85, 86
racing 34, 77–82
Royalty, acquisition by 122, 123, 128
speed achievable 32
tolls 87, 88
tour from London to Falkirk 65
tours on continent 65
Twentieth century machines 100
wagers and 'matches against
  time' 76, 77
Wales, hobby-horse in 43
widespread use 69
Hobby-horse prints:
Ackermann, Rudolph,
  publisher 146, 147
Alken, Henry, artist 146, 147, 174
*Anti-Dandy Infantry
  Triumphant* 152
A new Irish Jaunting Car 162, 166
A new Irish Jaunting Car,
  preliminary sketch for 162, 167
An Unexpected Occurrence 147
A Pilentum 137
*A P****e, Driving his Hobby,
  in HERDFORD!!!* 125, 126, 128
artist identification 172, 174
Boarding School Hobbies 153, 157
categorization of 146
Cruikshank, George,
  artist 161, 162, 172
Cruikshank, Robert,
  artist 161, 172, 174
Dandies on their Hobbies! 162, 164
Dandies on their Hobbies!,
  preliminary sketch for 165
Draisiennes dites Vélocipèdes 9–11
Dublin, prints published in 171

earliest and latest 145
*Economy – or a Duke of Ten
  Thousand* 123–126, 128
*Enough to make a Horse
  Laugh!* 159–161
Every Man on his Perch 26, 27
Every One His Hobby (two
  prints) 150, 154, 155, 158, 174
FASHIONABLE EXERCISE
  etc. 130, 131, 139
Going to the Races 150, 151
Heath, William, artist 147, 174
Hobby-Horse Fair (two
  prints) 173, 174, 188, 189
*Hobby-horses jockeying the
  Mail!!* 66, 67
Hudson, John, publisher 147
Humphrey, G., publisher 174
*Jack mounted on his Dandy
  Charger* 32
*Johnson's Pedestrian Hobbyhorse
  Riding School* 40, 42, 51, 104, 105, 131, 146, 147, 174
Johnson, the First Rider etc. –
  portrait of Johnson's son 52, 53, 146, 147
Marks, J.L., print shop
  publisher/artist 171, 174
Match against Time etc. 148, 149
Military Hobbyhorse 88, 89
Modern Olympics 77–79, 147
Modern Pegasus etc. 79, 80
*More Hobbies, or the Veloci
  Manipede* 140, 142, 147
*New Reading – or – Shakspeare
  Improved* 117, 119, 120
Pedestrian Hobbyhorse 66, 68, 146, 147
*Pedestrians Travelling
  on the New Invented
  Hobby-Horse!* 24–26

Perambulators in Hyde Park 72, 73
political satire 146, 167
public collections 145
relationship between artist, engraver, printer, publisher 169, 171
Rowlandson, Thomas – hobby-horse artist myth 174
R***L HOBBY'S!!! – pedals myth 179, 180
Sidebethem, James, publisher 159–162
Sievier's Patent Pedestrian Carriage 189–191
Stop him who can!! etc. – Johnson portrait 15, 16, 172
Tegg, Thomas, publisher 150, 159, 160
The Chancellors' Hobby etc. 167, 168
The Dandy Charger 105, 147, 148
The Devil alias Simon Pure 167, 169, 170
The Female Race etc. 87, 139, 140
The Hobby Horse Dealer 140, 141
The Master of the Ordnance exercising his Hobby 153, 156
The New Invented Sociable etc. 143, 144
The Ladies Hobby 136, 137
The Ladies Hobbye 147
The Parsons Hobby 109, 110
The Pedestrian Carriage, or Walking Accelerator 162, 163
The Radical Quaker – undiscovered print 169
The Rev. Joseph Coltman 110
types of print 146
Vélocipède Sentimental!! etc. 143
Views of the Lady's Pedestrian Hobbyhorse 131–134, 147

Williams, C., artist 174
'Yedis', artist 161, 174
Howell's 'Dicycle'-type machine 191–193
Hull, incident at 85
Hursley, fatal accident at 84
Hyde Park:
 attempted exhibition of hobby-horses 71
 extent of use in 34, 71–73
Ipswich:
 daily riding to Whitton 81
 racing at 79, 80
Ireland, the hobby-horse in 171, 172

Johnson, Denis:
 appointment of Leeds agent 57
 assignment of patent 55–57
 birth date and early life 13
 business premises in Long Acre 17
 character as revealed by Will 61, 62
 children of 14, 15
 commemorative plaque 17, 18
 continuation as coachmaker 61
 death and burial 61
 financial success, extent of 54
 firm, continuation of by Allen family 62, 63
 handwriting and signature 15
 improvements in Laufmaschine 18
 machines – *see* Hobby-horse
 manufacture and marketing by 49
 marriage to Mary Newman 13, 14
 partnership with John Allen 61
 patent 18–21
 patent infringement in Liverpool 57, 58
 portrait 15, 16

217

relationship with Samuel
   Merscy   56, 57
riding schools   51
suspected unauthorized
   copying of his machines   57, 58, 60, 61
visit to America   54
Will   61, 62
Johnson, John:
   expert rider of hobby-horse   52–54
   identity   52
   London exhibition   52
   portrait   52, 53
   tour of England   52
Jugs:
   depicting John Bull's velocipede   150, 151, 153
   depicting supposed tandem hobby-horse   125, 128
   large commemorative, with hobby-horse illustrations   158, 159

Karlsruhe:
   birthplace of von Drais   4
   monument erected to von Drais   12
Kean, Edmund, actor, depicted with hobby-horse   117, 119, 120
Kent, Mr, inventor of Marine Velocipede and Aquatic Tripod, or Tricipede   194, 195
Kerr, T., hobby-horse maker   128

Ladies' hobby-horse riding:
   evidence for   129, 140, 141, 143
   instructions for   129, 131
   riding school theory   130, 131
   suggestive depiction in prints   130, 139, 140
   unwillingness to participate in   131

Lady's Velocipede, treadled three-wheeler   139
Lady's version of Johnson hobby-horse   131–135
'Land punt', patented by Baynes   187, 188
Laufmaschine:
   Badenian privilege   9
   early use in Bath   12
   exhibition in Nancy   11
   exhibition in Paris   11
   first use in Germany   1
   first use in France   9, 11
   French patent   9, 19
   invention by von Drais   1
   journey over Pyrenees   65
Leeds:
   appointment of agent in   57
   Johnson's tour of England   52
Lees, Cottam & Hallen, makers of Sievier machine   189
Leicester, the hobby-horse in   71
Lewes:
   proposed racing at   79
   the hobby-horse at   70
Liskeard, 'match against time' ride to   77
Liverpool:
   accident at   54
   early invention of machine by B. Smythe   175
   Johnson's tour of England visits   54
   patent infringement in   57, 58
   velocipede manufacture in   57
London:
   accident in Waterloo Road   84
   early use of hobby-horse in   64
   hobby-horse hoax poem   74, 75
   hobby-horse journeys to Brighton   122, 123
   tour to Falkirk in Scotland   65

Index

Long Acre:
  Denis Johnson
    commemorative plaque   17, 18
  Johnson's premises at 75 Long
    Acre   17
Lowe, Robert, M.P., youthful
  hobby-horse rider   107, 108, 110

Machines – *see* Hobby-horse
  and Laufmaschine
Manchester:
  Johnson's tour of England,
    visit to   52
  racing at   81, 82
Manivelociter, manumotive
  machine   181–184
Mannheim:
  first use of Laufmaschine   1
  von Drais family move to   4
Mannheim Castle gardens, von
  Drais portrayed in   6
Manumotive machines of
  Charles Lucas Birch   181–184
Marine Velocipede, invention
  of Mr Kent   194
Marlborough, Duke of,
  hobby-horse owner   119
Merscy:
  assignee of Johnson patent   56
  relationship with Denis
    Johnson   56, 57
Metropolis Paving Act,
  prosecutions under   85, 86

Nancy, exhibition of
  Laufmaschine   1
New York, Johnson promoting
  machine   54
Nobility, acquisition and use of
  hobby-horses   34, 119, 121, 122

Northumberland, Duke of,
  hobby-horse incident   121
Norwich:
  Finch advert for hobby-horse
    instruction   69, 70
  Flying Actaeons at   187
  the hobby-horse at   76
Nottingham:
  race between hobby-horse and
    donkey   82
  the hobby-horse at   70

Oxford, the hobby-horse at   76

Palmer, John, mail coach
  service of   116
Paris, exhibition of Laufmaschine   11
Patent Pedestrian Carriage,
  Sievier's   189–191
Pedestrian Curricle – *see*
  Hobby-horse
Petersham, Lord, leading dandy
  & possible hobby-horse rider   104,
    105, 115
Pilentum, lady's three-wheel
  velocipede   134, 136–138, 174
Pilentum coach, whether
  actually existed   173
Pill box depicting hobby-horse
  riders   103
Playing card depicting
  hobby-horse rider   112
Plates depicting Pilentum   138
Prince Regent (later George IV):
  acquisition of Johnson
    machines   122, 125
  depiction as hobby-horse rider
    in prints   123, 125–127
  military use apparently
    considered by   210

219

relationships with titled ladies
   123, 125, 126, 128
Pyrenees, journey over from
   Pau to Madrid   65

Queen Anna Paulowna, owner
   of hobby-horse   127, 128

Riding schools   51
Royal College of Surgeons,
   interest in the velocipede   91, 92
Rutter, John, velocipede
   supplier   60, 61

Salomons, Sir David, bequest
   to Bibliothèque Nationale   145
Scotland, the hobby-horse in   34, 43
Seine, Bernhard, early user of
   Laufmaschine in Bath   12
Shaftesbury, velocipedes
   supplied at   59–61
Sheffield, hobby-horse racing at   82
Sheridan, Richard Brinsley,
   grandfather, politician,
   playwright   106, 107, 116
Sievier, inventor of Patent
   Pedestrian Carriage   189–191
Smythe, B., inventor of British
   Facilitator   175–177
Sociable, lady passenger
   machine, Continental origin
   of   143
Southampton, the hobby-horse at   90
Southern Veteran-Cycle Club,
   commemorative horse-brass   11
Spry, Rev. William, eccentric
   hobby-horse rider   111, 112

St. Columb, match against
   time, ride from   77
Steam, anticipated use of   183, 184

Theatrical interest in
   hobby-horse   114–117, 119
Tolls, hobby-horse riders'
   liability to pay   87, 88
Trivector, manumotive
   machine   182–184

Upstreet, 'match against time'
   from   77

Velocimanipede, lady passenger
   machine   140, 142, 143, 174, 179
Velocipede – *see* Hobby-horse
   and Laufmaschine
'Velocipede':
   contrasted with 'hobby-horse'   51
   French origin of term   2
'Velocipedi', supposed early use
   of word in Italy   2

Wales, the hobby-horse in   43
Whitton, daily riding to, from
   Ipswich   81
Wilcox, James, Hertfordshire
   velocipede artist   96, 97
Willem, Prince of Orange,
   owner of hobby-horse   127, 128
Woodstock, the hobby-horse at   76
Worthing, hobby-horse hoax   73

Yarmouth machine, pedals
   hypothesis   177–179